PROJECT
MANAGEMENT
FOR THE
UNOFFICIAL
PROJECT
MANAGER

Praise for *Project Management for the Unofficial Project Manager*

"In this book, Kory, Suzette, and James have created the ultimate blueprint for 'unofficial' project managers. You'll go from amateur to adept in seven easy chapters."
—Jay Wilkinson, founder and CEO of Firespring

"*Project Management for the Unofficial Project Manager* gets to the HEART of a challenge so many now face in the workplace—the need to ORGANIZE projects, on the fly, without training, to lead their companies to a new future. This is a GREAT book—Exceedingly Practical, Easy-To-Read, Personable, and Hits the Spot—you'll take control fast with the knowledge in these pages."
—Julie Morgenstern, *New York Times* bestselling author of *Time Management from the Inside Out*

"*Project Management for the Unofficial Project Manager* is the new benchmark for real & truly effective project management. This is a must-read ..."
—Gerry Aquino, Organizational Development and Learning at Össur Americas, Inc.

"*Project Management for the Unofficial Project Manager* is the best business improvement book that I have ever read. This book will become the guide for all of our future projects. We are already seeing massive improvements from the work sessions that Jim Wood conducted at our company, and this book will definitely enhance those improvements. Any person who follows the advice in this book will find a tremendous, positive impact on their career."

—Tim Rancourt, president of Engineering and Manufacturing at Northern Tool + Equipment

"Finally! A project management book that acknowledges and supports the 'people' part of projects. Too many times we are focused on the work without recognizing that it's people and relationships that have the biggest impact on project success. Practicing the Four Foundational Behaviors will help every 'unofficial' project manager engage their team."

—Deanna Carrera, director of Leadership and Learning at First Things First

"In this age of lean corporate headcount, everyone, no matter what their title, is required to fill the role of project manager. And the new book, *Project Management for the Unofficial Project Manager*, covers the core areas that any project professional needs to be successful. Additionally, FranklinCovey's work session gives you simple, straightforward, video-driven content that is easy to understand and put into practice. The book can also serve as a reinforcement tool to remind work session participants of their learning. Both are invaluable resources to any organization interested in improving efficiency and outcomes."

—Robert Fitt, senior director of Human Resources at Broadcom Corporation

"With *Project Management for the Unofficial Project Manager*, FranklinCovey has put project management in the hands of everyday leaders. The book provides practical solutions and a straightforward process to craft shared vision, realistic timelines, and successful deliverables. If you are involved with executing projects of any size, you owe it to yourself and your team to read this book."

— **Kenneth Johnson, director of Training and Development for the State of Colorado**

"Sometimes we think of projects as large capital expenditures, but often all of our work is an 'unofficial' project, and too often, we find ourselves ill-equipped to manage the process to a successful outcome. *Project Management for the Unofficial Project Manager* ties together a process that everyone can use for project work, as it is for all levels of an organization. One great takeaway from the book is, 'You must clarify a shared and measurable set of expectations.' Without this, a project has little chance of success, because projects are really all about people and their expectations."

—**Bonnie Stone, Centralized Learning and Development Manager for the Central Arizona Project**

"In today's environment, managers need to lead and complete difficult and multiple projects with limited resources. Authors Kogon, Blakemore, and Wood outline down-to-earth examples and techniques, essential to be successful in this day and age."

— **Michael Fung, former CFO of Walmart U.S.**

"In an era where collaboration is key, where everyone has a 'real job' to do, in addition to the projects that they are a part of, this book may actually save lives or certainly improve them! People are pulled in so many directions that this book enables the project manager to be highly organized and build authority and credibility. A well-organized project manager is a gift to any organization and will surely deliver extraordinary results."

— **Kevin K. Cushing, former CEO of Alphagraphics Inc.**

PROJECT
MANAGEMENT
FOR THE
UNOFFICIAL
PROJECT
MANAGER

KORY KOGON,
SUZETTE BLAKEMORE,
AND JAMES WOOD

A FRANKLINCOVEY BOOK

BenBella Books, Inc.
Dallas, Texas

BENBELLA
BenBella Books, Inc.
10300 N. Central Expressway
Suite #530
Dallas, TX 75231
www.benbellabooks.com
Send feedback to feedback@benbellabooks.com

Printed in the United States of America
10 9 8 7 6 5 4 3 2 1

Library of Congress Cataloging-in-Publication Data
Kogon, Kory.
  Project management for the unofficial project manager / Kory Kogon, Suzette Blakemore, James Wood.
    pages cm
  "Franklin Covey book."
    ISBN 978-1-941631-10-2 (paperback) — ISBN 978-1-941631-11-9 (electronic) 1.
Project management. I. Title.
  HD69.P75K657 2015
  658.4'04—dc23

2014040744

Editing by Debbie Harmsen
Copyediting by James Fraleigh
Proofreading by Michael Fedison
  and Lisa Story
Indexing by Clive Pyne Book
  Indexing Services

Front cover design by Bradford Foltz
Full cover design by Sarah Dombrowsky
Text design by Silver Feather Design
Text composition by Integra Software
  Services Pvt. Ltd.
Printed by Lake Book Manufacturing

Distributed by Perseus Distribution (www.perseusdistribution.com)

To place orders through Perseus Distribution:
Tel: (800) 343-4499 / Fax: (800) 351-5073
E-mail: orderentry@perseusbooks.com

Significant discounts for bulk sales are available. Please contact Glenn Yeffeth at glenn@benbellabooks.com or (214) 750-3628.

Contents

INTRODUCTION: BATTLE SCARRED AND READY FOR A NEW APPROACH?

THIS BOOK HAS THREE AUTHORS. Two of us, Suzette and Kory, are "unofficial" project managers. We've been involved in projects throughout our careers, and we're both accomplished and battle scarred. As successful as we were in our early careers at implementing marketing programs, rolling out learning programs, and managing a global installation of ISO 9000, we realize now that if we had just known how to apply a simple methodology to the work, we might have avoided a few scars. Fortunately, our projects turned out well, but not without a high degree of stress, unnecessary sacrifices, missed deadlines, re-work, and tears along the way—most of which we could have dodged had we known a few project management basics.

Now, as we research productivity in the twenty-first-century workplace, we realize that the methods and systems that "official" project managers use can fill an enormous skills gap for what has become the unofficial project management workforce—basically the vast majority of knowledge workers. Most knowledge workers are managing projects under the radar—everything from micro-projects to extremely large macro-projects—and doing so by the seat of their pants! Because most knowledge workers are driven and talented, they push through pretty well despite a lack of project management skills, although, like us, not without a few scars. Lucky for us, business maven and certified Project Management Professional James Wood brought his official project management expertise to our research, helping us to distill the best ideas from that world and make them usable and practical for all of us "regular" people. As a result, we've taught thousands of unofficial project managers a basic method for project success, and now we're sharing what we've learned with you.

One of FranklinCovey's clients, a director in his company's Project Management Office, has this to say about our program and tools for the unofficial project manager: "In the last year, our company has overspent on projects by $2.5 million. And the reason is not the 'Big P' projects. The 'Big P' projects have plenty of oversight and corrective action when needed. The greater challenge is the everyday, 'Small P' projects. While these projects are small in scope, there are hundreds of them—and no one is paying attention. The big payoff for conducting FranklinCovey's program *Project Management Essentials for the Unofficial Project Manager* is not to get better project success, but to save millions of dollars in our internal expense budget!"

WHY THIS BOOK

This book is for those of us who are paid to think, innovate, and create. It's for those of us who are asked to "get 'er done."

It's for those of us who are movers and shakers at work and at home. We're known to make things happen, and we get stuff done no matter what. There are many tools and plenty of illustrations to help you understand the material, but this book is neither a comprehensive textbook nor a reference guide. It teaches you the essentials in a real-world manner. We show you how to manage a project through real-life stories about unofficial project managers like you who have applied this approach to get their work done with greater ease, excellence, and predictability.

Interestingly, we've found that this unofficial project-management method has positive side effects. It complements and augments the critical time- and life-management skills we must use to excel in the über-paced, chaotic, and information-overloaded environment of the twenty-first century. Apply the method to your own work and home lives. Follow the principles consistently, and you will unlock your potential for even greater accomplishment.

WHAT TO EXPECT

Each chapter starts with a critical mindset you must adopt in order to apply the methodology, followed by an essential skillset and toolset. If the stories and principles ring true to you, we have no doubt you will find the purpose and passion needed to master the skillset and make it an unconscious competency in yourself and in the people you lead. Digest and chuckle at our "Project Management Proverbs," and ask yourself the "Check Your Learning" questions at the end of each chapter.

This book is about going from good to great in both your professional and personal lives. It is about learning to execute your highest-quality work—whether you're taking on a huge professional project or feeling pressured to plan a perfect wedding. By consistently practicing what this book advocates, you will be able to repeat success over and over, avoiding most of the scars that project managers usually get along the way.

CHAPTER 1

The New World of "Unofficial" Project Management

Are you an unofficial project manager?

Before answering, consider what a project is:

PROJECT: *A temporary endeavor with a start and finish undertaken to create a unique product, service, or result.*

In our consulting work with clients across the globe, we've asked thousands of individuals this question: How much of your professional life is spent working on projects? Most clients say that between 60 and 80 percent of their time at work is project based. But when we ask if their job title is "project manager," virtually 100 percent answer with a resounding "No!" They say they are anything *but* project managers. And when we ask if they've ever been given project management training to handle that 60 to 80 percent of their time at work, very few hands go up. The vast majority say they've never had a single day of formal project management training. We call these people unofficial project managers.

> If most of your work time is spent on projects and you've never been exposed to formal project management training, you are an unofficial project manager.

So, if much of your day is spent working on projects, you, too, are an unofficial project manager. And you're not alone. A lot of us have quietly slipped into that role, and we're fighting project failure every day as we try to push through to a deadline, save a budget, or keep people (or ourselves) from messing everything up.

In fact, we don't usually succeed. According to the Project Management Institute (PMI), based in Newtown Square, Pennsylvania, and one of the world's largest professional associations, which sets industry standards for managing projects:

- Only 8 percent of organizations are "high performers" in managing projects.
- 45 percent of projects are either overdue or canceled altogether.
- Only 45 percent of projects actually meet the goals they're supposed to meet.
- For every US$100 invested in projects worldwide, there's a net loss of US$13.50—"lost forever—unrecoverable."[1]

THERE IS HOPE

If you've failed, if you haven't been happy with the process, or if you feel like your projects work but could be better, you might think you just need to "try harder." But your problems aren't due to a lack of trying. Without the right mindset, skillset, and toolset, you can't achieve real project success.

So how do you get those things? Well, the first thing to do—as you have done—is to pick up a book on project management.

There are literally hundreds of books on the market that will teach you how to manage a project. Most of them are written from the point of view of an official, formal, "real" project manager, while the rest contain intimidating, extremely complicated processes and specialized language.

So you pick up a book on project management, read a few chapters, pretend to "get" the formulas and definitions, read a few more chapters, then slowly but steadily become overwhelmed, and finally you just panic. At this point, you begin to doubt if you're smart enough or patient enough to really get it. So you shut the cover, put the book on the shelf (or delete it forever), and say to yourself, "Well, I've been doing okay up until now; I guess I'll just continue to wing it." Meanwhile your workload as an unofficial project manager keeps increasing—which means you'll keep feeling more and more pressure to lead and manage projects effectively.

But this book is different. It's based on two ideas:

1. Project management is the work of the twenty-first century. This means that everyone is a project manager.

2. Project management is no longer just about managing a process. It's also about leading people—twenty-first-century people. This is a significant paradigm shift. It's about tapping into the potential of the people on the team, then engaging with and inspiring them to offer their best to the project.

You're not likely to find these ideas in other books on project management. By contrast, this book contains a reliable, proven formula to help you manage projects and lead people in *this* century—people who are *knowledge* workers, who bring their *minds* to the job, who are volunteers you can't and won't be able to control. (They probably don't work for you anyway, right?)

Learn from Failure

Before we go any further, let's understand why projects fail. According to the PMI, organizations with few formal project management processes in place (what the PMI calls low-maturity organizations)[2] are far more likely to experience project failure than companies that follow a process. But even high-maturity organizations fail much of the time. Here are the most common reasons for failure that we hear about:

- lack of commitment/support
- unrealistic timelines
- too many competing priorities
- unclear outcomes/expectations
- unrealistic resources
- people pulled away from the project
- politics/legislation
- lack of a "big picture" for the team
- poor planning
- lack of leadership
- changing standards
- lack of or mismanaged budget

Do these problems look familiar? People from all over the world are facing the same issues. And they come with a price tag. Again according to the PMI, a failed project costs an additional one-third of the original budget. Whether you are responsible for a multimillion-dollar project or a series of thousand-dollar projects, failure is expensive!

And there are even greater costs than just the budget. What about lost opportunities? Dissatisfied customers? Loss of innovation? And, most damaging, diminished employee engagement and morale? People often end projects wondering if they've made any real contribution. When a project fails, the project managers (including unofficial ones) come off as incompetent. Morale goes down and disengagement goes up. Over time, many organizations struggle to get even the simplest projects completed with excellence.

According to the PMI, in low-maturity organizations, only:

- 39 percent of projects get done on time.
- 44 percent are completed on budget.
- 53 percent meet the original intent or business purpose.

Learn from Success

Now that we've seen why projects fail, let's look closely at why they succeed. A successful project:

- meets or exceeds expectations,
- optimizes resources, and
- builds team confidence and morale for future projects.

Too many people call your project a success if all you've done is meet the deadline and the budget. But did you meet or exceed expectations, the first measure of success? Did you achieve your business outcomes? Did you meet your quality objectives? And did you truly optimize resources, the second measure of success? Many project managers say they finish their projects on time and on budget, but they also confess that the quality, completeness, or outcomes of their projects suffer in the end. Then the third measure of success, morale, is often left out of the picture. Yet what's more valuable to your future than a confident team eager to move on to the next success?

In today's lean and mean, globally competitive world, you're expected to optimize resources, do more with less, and deliver on time and with excellent quality. Whether you're an official or unofficial project manager, you can't afford *not* to find and use methods that maximize your human, technical, and budgetary resources.

> Too many people call your project a success if all you've done is meet the deadline and the budget. But did you meet or exceed expectations, the first measure of success? Did you achieve your business outcomes? ... And did you truly optimize resources, the second measure of success?

MANAGE PROJECTS, LEAD PEOPLE

In this book, we use "project manager" and "project leader" interchangeably—if you're going to be effective, you need to be good at both. When you're in charge of a project, you manage *things*—deliverables, deadlines, schedules, and scope—but you also lead *people*—team members, customers, consultants, and yes, even "higher-ups." Your role in leading people is to inspire them to follow you and the project management process willingly and enthusiastically.

Project management is as much about effectively leading people as it is about skillfully managing a process. You've heard the fable of the goose and the golden eggs—you'll recall that the impatient farmer killed the goose to get at all the eggs and ended up with nothing. In project management terms, the outcome is the golden egg, but the project team is the goose. The true formula for winning at projects is PEOPLE + PROCESS = SUCCESS.

Me, a Leader?

"But I'm not a leader. I'm not even a manager," you say. We hear you. Here's a story about a project manager who didn't think he was a leader . . . until he had to become one.

"Manage things. Lead people."
—STEPHEN R. COVEY

When famous marketing guru Seth Godin was young, he agreed to lead a project at work. He himself was totally committed, but he worried about the commitment level of his small, struggling company and the team of three helpers assigned to him.

So he started a newsletter that "highlighted the work of every person" on the team. "It highlighted their breakthroughs and talked about the new ground we were breaking. I made photocopies and distributed the newsletter to every person in the company. Twice a week I talked about our quest. Twice a week, I chronicled the amazing work of our tiny tribe . . . Within a month, six engineers had defected to the tribe working with me . . . Then it was twenty." Eventually, thirty people were eating and sleeping and working around the clock on Seth's team, and within months they shipped products that saved the company.

As he explains, "They switched for the journey. They wanted to be part of something that mattered . . . Twenty years later people on that team still talk about what we built. And I, the twenty-four-year-old with no experience and no staff, got to go on the ride of a lifetime."[3]

Why was Seth able to draw such committed people around himself? *Because he valued them.* People naturally want to *matter*—and they want to make a contribution that matters.

Just because you can describe a project management process doesn't mean you can lead people successfully through it. How often have you wished other people were as motivated as you—that you could push them to do better? In today's knowledge worker world, you cannot "push" anyone to do "better." They must *want* to volunteer their best efforts, and you must be their inspiration.

Me, a Project Manager?

While some are nervous about leading people, you may be the opposite—great with people, but anxious about the process part. If so, relax. Project management is not rocket science. Although the project management profession has collected a huge body of knowledge on the subject and devised complex computer applications for it, you'll find the basic elements easy to grasp. "Whether it's a $50,000 study or a $30 billion 'giga' project, the basic tenets of project management should not change," says one professional.[4]

So you don't need to make the job more complicated than it is. One project management pro explains that if you keep the simple things straight, you'll be okay. He says, "Most complex projects fail because [the managers] forgot the very simple things, not because they couldn't deal with complexity."[5]

Simple is good. In fact, you might be better off without the vast machinery that the project management profession uses. As we said, there is a fairly well-understood process for managing a project, one that the PMI defines in detail. Throughout this book you'll see quotations from PMI's *Guide to the Project Management Body of Knowledge (PMBOK)*[6] so you'll know where the principles we're teaching you came from.

Founded in 1969, the Project Management Institute (PMI) sets standards for the project management profession. It has 454,000 members in 180 countries.

We've narrowed down PMI's robust process to the essentials and added our own insights about what makes projects successful. According to the PMI, there are five "process groups." Technically, they're not supposed to be "steps" or "phases" in managing the project, but it might be easier to think of them that way. They are the following:

1. Initiate
2. Plan
3. Execute
4. Monitor and Control
5. Close

In the chapters that follow, you'll learn more about these five process groups and the mindsets, skillsets, and toolsets you can adopt to achieve project success. You'll also learn how to lead and inspire others on your team to play to win big. In the next chapter, we'll explore how to use the PEOPLE + PROCESS = SUCCESS formula to create highly successful projects.

TO SUM UP 🎧

Projects have become the workflow of the twenty-first century. Knowledge workers at all levels have quietly slipped into the role of "unofficial project manager," relying on their experience and their wits to get through to a decent finish. It's often like trying to fly an airplane without flying lessons. As a result, the list of project failures is long, pervasive, frustrating, and very costly both personally and organizationally.

PEOPLE + PROCESS is the key paradigm shift for twenty-first-century project management. By mastering informal authority and a few practical processes, you can become a consistently successful unofficial project manager.

CHECK YOUR LEARNING— UNOFFICIAL PROJECT MANAGEMENT

✓ What are some differences between official and unofficial project managers?

✓ Why do fewer than half of all projects actually meet their goals?

✓ What are the signs of a successful project?

✓ What does it mean to "manage projects" but to "lead people"?

✓ "Whether it's a $50,000 study or a $30 billion 'giga' project, the basic tenets of project management should not change." What's true about that statement?

CHAPTER 2

PEOPLE + PROCESS = SUCCESS

HAVE YOU EVER HEARD YOURSELF say, "I'm a process person," or "I'm a people person"? Some people naturally thrive on the operations side, while others love engaging, inspiring, and leading people.

One of our consultants, Dave, illustrated this point when he asked a group of people if they felt more aligned to the people side or the process side of project management. He asked the participants who were "people people" to walk to one side of the room, and those who were "process people" to walk to the other side of the room. At first, it looked like no one was going to the people side. But after a minute, a handful of men and women trickled over.

"Okay 'process people,' look across the room," Dave said. "This group sees themselves as 'people people.' They value teamwork, engagement, and morale. Who would like to give an example of why process is so important?"

Without hesitation, one man burst out, "Process is the *most* important thing." He was adamant. "Follow it!"

Another person declared, "When all else fails, return to the process!"

Dave interrupted, "I can see you feel very, very strongly about this." The people in the room laughed a little.

Then Dave turned to the other group. "For a moment, I thought no one was going to head this way. I can't help but notice there are only a few of you on this side of the room. Why?"

The group was quiet, and then one of the senior leaders spoke up: "In an organization full of engineers, being a 'people person' is not always valued or appreciated." He smiled and glanced nervously at the large group across the room, then turned back to the consultant.

"I understand," Dave said. "So, if you could tell these 'process people' who value tasks, data, and tracking just one thing, what would you say about how important people are to the project?"

This time the senior leader answered with the same conviction his process colleague had shown earlier. "Well, it won't matter how good your process is if you can't engage a group of good people to run it."

When the senior leader shared his "aha!" moment, the rest of the group started to relax, acknowledged their own biases, and opened their minds to both sides of the project management formula:

People + Process

If you had been in the room that day, which side would you have gone to? If you are a "people person," it's highly likely that following a process is not your favorite thing. If you are someone who loves a good process, you might find yourself struggling when you have to manage people. Becoming aware of your own preference is a good start to opening yourself to new possibilities. It's the first step to becoming effective at both—because both, in fact, are needed.

In the official project management world, too many people focus solely on the project management *process* when leading a project. And unfortunately, the unofficial project manager follows suit. They both have a blind spot when it comes to leading the people involved in making the project succeed. Their prevailing mindset is this formula:

Process = Success

A great process is one key to great project success, but the process is only half of the equation. The other half of the formula—equally important as the first half—is leading people:

People + Process = Success

The unofficial project manager who adopts the mindset of PEOPLE + PROCESS knows the secret to project success and can replicate it over and over again.

LEAD THE PEOPLE

Once upon a time, people didn't think much about the human side of project management. But research has caught up with today's reality. "In the 1980s, we believed that the failure of a project was largely a quantitative failure due to ineffective planning, scheduling, estimating, cost control, and 'moving targets,'" says Harold Kerzner, a top researcher in the field of project management. "During the 1990s, we changed our view of failure from being quantitatively oriented to qualitatively oriented." The thinking now is that failure can be "largely attributed to poor morale, poor motivation, poor human relations, poor productivity, [and] no employee commitment."[1]

Managing the process with excellence is important, but being a good leader is *essential*. Enforcing project management techniques can never substitute for motivating and empowering people to implement them themselves. You want people to work with you, not against you. You've somehow got to inspire your team to fully commit to the project and motivate them to follow the process if you're going to achieve long-term success.

Why? Because efficiency and control strategies rarely work—especially in the long run. If you're an official project manager or boss, you may be able to coax people into being productive, but rarely can you force them to bring their most creative energy and efforts to a project. And as an unofficial project manager, you often lack the formal authority to tell anyone what to do. For instance, do the people on your project team report to you? In many cases, they don't. Can you order people to perform? Probably not. To have real project success, you need what we call "informal authority."

> Informal authority inspires people to want to play on your team and win.

Formal versus Informal Authority

Formal authority comes from a title or a position. Giving people titles doesn't necessarily make them good leaders. A title may allow someone to enforce rules or penalize team members when rules aren't followed, but titles alone rarely guarantee willing followers who cheerfully volunteer their best talent and effort.

In contrast, informal authority comes from the character and capabilities of a leader. For example, Mahatma Gandhi never held a formal position, yet he led India to independence and inspired movements for civil rights and freedom across the world. Nelson Mandela and Martin Luther King Jr. didn't have official leadership titles, yet from their prison cells they inspired, empowered, and effectively led people.

Each of these leaders earned the right to influence through informal authority because they inspired trust due to their strong character and integrity. Informal authority can be far more powerful than formal authority.

For example, think of a person you have worked with in the past—a coworker, friend, teacher, or informal leader—who inspired you to give your best. Would you say he or she had informal authority? What was it about the person that made you want to contribute? In what ways did she or he motivate you? By a good example? By listening well? By showing you and others respect? How did that person hold you accountable for results that motivated you to perform?

"Character is who you are under pressure, not when everything is fine."
—RITU GHATOURY

You may not be leading a social movement like Gandhi or Mandela, but as a project manager you will need to inspire people to want to play on your team, contribute fully, and do their best work. Whether or not you hold a formal position of authority, you can become a true leader if you behave like one. Like the leaders just mentioned, you will need strong character and integrity, and the people you lead must feel respected and heard. As each member of your team will have differing needs, personalities, work styles, and talents, they will need you to be consistent in your approach to their needs and the project process.

Four Foundational Behaviors

Through our work with hundreds of clients over the years, we've identified Four Foundational Behaviors that will help you earn the informal authority you need to engage people fully to achieve the expected project outcomes. While we could have chosen dozens of leadership behaviors to focus on, we have found that mastering these four can make all the difference:

1. Demonstrate respect
2. Listen first
3. Clarify expectations
4. Practice accountability

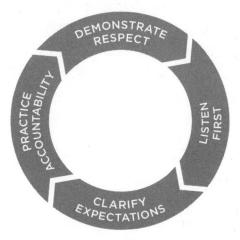

We will touch on each behavior briefly here, but we'll return to them often because they're so crucial to every part of the project management process.

DEMONSTRATE RESPECT

One young engineer says of his project manager, "Even though we are in such a fast-paced environment, Jennifer works hard to provide us a fair amount of lead time to accomplish something. She's always thinking in advance of what's going to happen. She's been known to bring in lunch if we have a looming critical deadline. Sometimes she asks us to do the impossible, but she takes the time to explain why. Just knowing helps us find a 'little extra' to do the 'impossible.' These little things make all the difference to how we feel about working with Jennifer.

"When it's crunch time, when things get crazy and it's harder to demonstrate respect, Jennifer becomes more respectful, not less. She demonstrates this respect by anticipating problems and meeting the team's needs. The more respected team members feel, even when having a tough conversation, the more engaged they will be."

Showing respect does not mean becoming a doormat. Like Jennifer, you can hold people accountable while being respectful by talking straight with them. In fact, straight talk is a form of respect, if you're considerate about it and consistently practice it with everyone at every level—from the people on your team to the key stakeholders and even the top executives.

Think of a time in your life when someone you respected confronted reality and talked straight with you. Even if it was a little painful in the moment, you probably digested the feedback and made a few changes.

Respect is its own reward. If you're honest with yourself and others, if you hold on to your integrity, you've succeeded regardless of the outcome. Generally, though, if you respect others, they'll respect you, and you'll be pleased with the outcome.

Listen First

Depending on your idea of what a project manager does, you might operate under the false assumption that you have to know everything. After all, you're in charge. You're expected to have all the answers. You've got to know at every moment if every last piece of the project is on budget, on time, or going as expected, right? After all, if the project doesn't go well, you'll be the one who faces the consequences.

This pressure to know it all may tempt you to talk more than listen. Your instinct to "tell, tell, tell" may kick in out of fear. If you don't have the answer—especially the right answer—people might find out how little you really know. Or, if you listen attentively to someone who may be struggling or complaining, you might hear about a problem you don't truly want to face. These reactions are understandable. They're also potentially fatal.

So it's crucial to resist that temptation to talk more than listen. Failure to listen can lead to strained relationships, decreased productivity, missed learning opportunities, and damaging errors in judgment.

Imagine going to a doctor with a pain in your stomach. She hands you a pill without even trying to hear you out or diagnosing the root of the problem—"Take this pill and you'll be fine. Next patient!" You might have stomach cancer or simple indigestion, but she'll never know.

When people come to you with complaints, problems, or requests for changes, let them talk first. Don't let the project blow up because you don't have the patience or maturity to hear people out *before* you decide what to do. Don't jump in with your solution right away. Make sure you understand the problem first.

But I'm moving too fast. I don't have time to listen, you might be thinking. Yes, project deadlines are looming, and the pressure to perform is great. But slowing down to listen may actually speed things up. If your response to team members who want to talk is, "Not now, I don't have time," they may slink back to work thinking, *She doesn't even listen to a thing I say,* or, *He doesn't respect me.* Listening first is inextricably tied to demonstrating respect. When you fail to listen, you automatically send out a clear signal of disrespect. Imagine how much time it will take to repair the trust and respect levels you just lost by failing to listen. Imagine how long it might take to rebuild that relationship and reengage those team members to give their finest effort.

If you are smart, you'll resist the temptation to talk more than listen. You'll realize that no one person can possibly have all the answers all of the time. The entire team, not just you, is responsible for the project's success. While your job is to manage the process, more importantly it is also to inspire the people. And inspiring starts when you listen first, then talk later.

One straight-talking project leader says, "If you are truly interested in building a high-performance team, get to know them. Ask them to be honest about their feelings. Ask them to be honest about what truly motivates and inspires them. Ensure them that you will not judge their answers. Share with them what motivates and inspires you. Create a family unity."[2]

The key principle at work here is *empathy*. If you have empathy, you don't have to agree or disagree with the people talking with you, but you put yourself in their place and work hard at understanding where they're coming from. When you give others the chance to express what's on their minds, to explain, or just to vent—*without interrupting*—you make the relationship stronger.

Don't be the one who doesn't care what they say. Don't be the one who panics when they have a problem. Instead, let them keep talking! Have you ever noticed that people often solve their own problems just by talking them through? Let team members grow; don't take all the responsibility for solving everything on yourself.

CLARIFY EXPECTATIONS

Most of the talking you do as a project leader is to clarify expectations. One of the main jobs of an unofficial project manager is to get everyone "on the same page," as they say. This is not easy, and it's the biggest potential pitfall you will face as a project leader.

Ask ten people what a "great vacation" consists of, and you'll get at least twenty different answers. Everyone has different expectations. To compound matters, not only do people disagree with each other, but they also change their own minds. People second-guess themselves constantly. They tell you what they want one minute and then contradict it the next. It's just the way humans work.

As a project leader, you're stuck with this reality.

But informal authority means constantly and consistently clarifying both the specific *and* the overall expectations for your team members. Many times we hear project managers say to individual team members, "Just do your task. Don't worry about the rest." These project managers think they do you a favor by offering an easy road, but what you hear is, "You are not capable, you are not valued. Make your component, compile your list. Just put your head down and do the job." Team members end up feeling disrespected and with a limited idea of the project's big-picture outcome. You don't know what contribution you're making. You may not be clear about the purpose you serve on the team. You've been relegated to a "job," not a contribution to a bigger whole.

But feeling like you're making a contribution is what makes you excited and confident.

If you really want to inspire a team to play and win big, keep them informed. Clearly communicate how each person's role contributes to the whole. Even small tasks can make a huge impact on the project's ultimate success, and a clear "big picture" is a surefire way to keep people engaged.

Stephen R. Covey once said, "The cause of almost all relationship difficulties is rooted in conflicting or ambiguous expectations around roles and goals."[3] As a project leader, your job is to communicate progress and clarify expectations. We'll look at this more in chapter three.

PRACTICE ACCOUNTABILITY

What do we mean by accountability?

Accountability as a project leader means that you are a model of excellence. You behave the way you want others to behave. The days of "do what I say, not what I do" are over. To inspire people to give you their best, they must see you "walk your talk."

Of course, you need to hold more than just yourself accountable. You must hold the entire team accountable to the standards you have set up. If Mary shows up late two or three times to the project meeting and she experiences no consequences, what do the team members learn about your ability to hold people accountable? What will they think and do in the future? Perhaps they might think, *Well, if Mary came in late and nothing happened, maybe I'll show up late, too.* Without standards of accountability in place, you are on the path to failure.

The first three behaviors—demonstrating respect, listening first, and clarifying expectations—are essential to maintaining accountability. The more you respect and listen to your team, and the clearer the expectations, the more your team members will hold themselves accountable, and the more informal authority you will earn to be able to hold them accountable. Unless you practice the first three behaviors, your attempts to hold people accountable will fail.

"A project manager is a master in the art of Done," says one expert. "If there is an obstacle in the path to Done, we remove it. Or we talk to the person or the people who can remove the obstacle. We bug them until they remove it. Then we repeat for the next obstacle. And then again. Over and over. Relentlessly. Until we reach Done. Then, and only then, do we stop. And, being masters in the art of Done, we stand up in front of a group of people and we say 'You can count on me. I will do this.' And we mean it."[4]

> Good project managers admit mistakes; that's why you so rarely meet a good project manager.

Accountability means transparency. When you report a status update, you tell it like it is. When you mess up, you admit it and take responsibility for it. The old saying "The truth hurts" isn't true. *Covering up the truth* is what hurts in the long run. We'll talk more about accountability in chapter five.

CHARACTER COUNTS

The Four Foundational Behaviors are not surface behaviors. If they don't arise from your inner character, you're putting up a façade, and people will know it. People are afraid of failing, of looking less than competent, of being blamed if things go wrong. A lot is at stake with a business project—the livelihood and self-image of real people are at stake, and you and they know it.

Without the inner character of a true leader, you can be a master of the process and still fail. In the words of one professional project manager, your project will be like a watermelon: "nice on the outside and one big mess once you cut through the surface."[5]

So who goes first? Who is going to be the model of excellence? It starts with the project leader's character—*your* character.

As a project leader, you're accountable for other people—for their hopes, their contributions, and their feelings of worth and achievement. You are also accountable for their mistakes, and you're accountable to your own conscience. But if you practice the Four Foundational Behaviors, then people will be able to count on you, and you'll be able to count on them and yourself.

According to the Project Management Institute, "focusing on the talent" should be the project leader's top priority.[6] That's a big, wide priority, but you can narrow it down to making sure that you practice these Four Behaviors and that others do, too—as we'll see a little later.

MANAGE THE PROCESS: THE FIVE PROCESS GROUPS

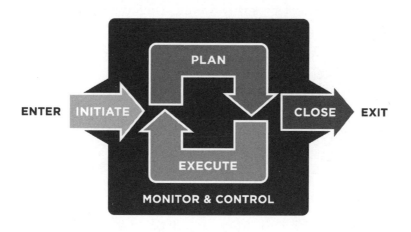

When we introduced the five process groups in chapter one, you, like many other people, may have asked yourself, "Does every project have to run through all five? What about the really small projects? Surely we can skip a few steps on small projects to save time."

Just to be clear, *every* successfully completed project runs through all five process groups. Of course, you complete the process groups a lot faster on a small project.

Did you know you already do these steps intuitively? For example, have you ever had to print something at your local copy shop? Perhaps a lost-dog flyer or an invitation to an event? If you have done this, you know exactly how the process goes.

You walk in with your document and someone meets you at the order counter. The project has begun. You've just entered **Initiate**. A customer service clerk takes your order and interviews you to clarify expectations. She asks you questions like, "How many do you want? Where will this be used? What color of paper? Double sided or single sided?" As you answer, she compiles the data into a clear Project Scope Statement.

Next she turns to confer with the machine operator, and your project has entered **Plan**. Together, they determine which machines should be used based on your requirements, the type of ink, and any binding that is needed. When they have finished planning, they will tell you how long your project will take.

Now, to **Execute**. Your project goes into the machine. The machine operator pushes a few buttons. Your item is being produced. While it is running, **Monitor and Control** comes into play. Someone will watch what is produced in order to get the highest-quality results. He will monitor things like whether the image is centered and the right ink colors and paper are being used. If you are still at the counter, a good operator will even walk over and ask you to confirm that everything is just as you expected.

Finally, when the project is complete, you enter **Close**. The customer service clerk asks you to sign off on the project and pay your bill. She might even ask for your contact information to store with your files so that the data can be found if you ever need to execute the project again.

One small project, done in a few minutes, carefully followed each of the five process groups.

So back to the question: Should every project be processed through all five groups? The answer is "Yes!" These processes aren't meant to make your project harder or take more time. In fact, if you follow them correctly, the five process groups will simplify the project, increase its speed and quality, and provide you with a reliable routine that will help you repeat success every time.

Let's look more deeply into the five process groups.

Initiate

At this stage you make sure everyone is clear about how project success will be measured. This is not an easy task. To clarify expectations, you'll get as much input as you can from your stakeholders—especially key stakeholders—to make sure everyone is on the same page.

Plan

Here you figure out exactly what needs to be delivered. Based on your deliverables, you create a well-defined budget, timelines, and project schedule.

Execute

Here you engage the team regularly to make sure everyone is on track. If you have initiated and planned your project well, executing your project will be much easier.

Monitor and Control

In every phase of your project, you will consistently monitor and control progress. You will make sure everything is going as expected, and if something gets off track, you will handle the required changes. You communicate your progress to key stakeholders. This isn't so much a singular step in the process as an ongoing effort that surrounds all the other process groups in the diagram.

Close

As you close your project, you check the results against the desired outcome. You recognize the team and document lessons learned. Closing a project will ensure that you and your team keep getting better and better.

FIVE PROCESS GROUPS

Project management processes can be organized into five groups of one or more processes each:

- Initiating processes authorizing the project.
- Planning processes defining and refining objectives . . .
- Executing processes coordinating people and resources to carry out the plan.
- Monitoring/controlling processes ensuring that objectives are met.
- Closing processes formalizing acceptance of the project.

—PMBOK 3.2

There is, of course, a lot more to project management than these five process groups, but for unofficial project managers, if you filter out the complexities, these are the essentials. In this book we've pared down these essentials so that someone with little or minimal skill and experience can successfully manage a project. In the following chapters we'll show you how to apply each of the five process groups in depth.

The rest of this book is organized around the Five Process Groups. Each process group chapter starts with a mindset, a principled paradigm you must adopt to execute the skillsets with power. You'll also be introduced to the toolset you'll need. You'll follow the stories of three people who are leading important projects and learn from them what works and what doesn't.

By the end of the book, you'll be well equipped to carry out your own projects successfully.

To get the most out of this book, apply what you learn to your own project. If you don't currently have a project, invent one to practice on. Use the steps, experiment with the tools, and you'll start to recognize the feelings associated with real project success!

TO SUM UP ☊

People + Process = Success

The Four Foundational Behaviors are sound, but they are not always simple. Picture this: You're on the verge of missing your project deadline. You're afraid there's no way to recover. You're off budget, and you've got people showing up at meetings unprepared (or not showing up at all). You've got an executive who wants to change everything, and you've got a boss screaming, "I expected this to be done! What's going on? Why can't you get control of this?"

Under this kind of pressure, it takes work, discipline, and practice to keep your head and inspire others to keep theirs.

We'll revisit the Four Behaviors throughout the book to see how they dramatically influence virtually every step of the project. Practice them until they become habits! If you don't, you'll get caught up in managing the process, forget to lead the people, and ultimately suffer project failure.

To paraphrase Aristotle, leadership requires both technical excellence *and* moral living. That's why your success depends on the Five Process Groups *plus* the Four Behaviors.

CHECK YOUR LEARNING— PEOPLE + PROCESS = SUCCESS

✓ What are some differences between formal and informal authority? Why is informal authority so important to the unofficial project manager?

✓ What are the Four Foundational Behaviors of a person with informal authority? Why are they "foundational"?

✓ "Focusing on the talent should be the project manager's top priority." What are some of the implications of that statement?

CHAPTER 3

INITIATING THE PROJECT: MOVE AHEAD OR GO AROUND IN CIRCLES?

INITIATE Mindset:
You must clarify a shared and measurable set of expectations.

T RY AN EXPERIMENT: BLINDFOLD SOME people, take them to a park, and ask them to walk forward in a straight line. What happens?

They walk in circles. Invariably. Sometimes the circles are wide, sometimes tight. The circles aren't perfect circles—they're loopy, sometimes in one direction, sometimes another. A lot of people even backtrack. Location doesn't matter either. This experiment has been tried around the world—on mountains, on beaches, in the Sahara Desert, even in the forests of Germany.[1]

But the point is, blindfolded people will never walk in a straight line.

Why is this? Apparently, we all walk in circles when we can't see a point of reference like the sun, the moon, a mountaintop, or a milestone. Without these things to refer to, we can't move forward.

That's why project management is so important. Without project management discipline, we lose direction. We lack the map, the landmarks, the milestones—all the things that keep us on track. So instead, we and our projects go around in circles. Because we aren't clear on expectations, we act like we're blindfolded. With only a general idea of which direction to go, we end up "circling back"—doing extra work (re-work), second-guessing, or getting smothered by "scope creep," which is the tendency of a project to change and grow into an uncontrollable monster.

SCOPE CREEP: *The tendency of a project to change and grow into an uncontrollable monster.*

In this chapter, you'll find out how to initiate a project so you move ahead rather than in circles. You'll see just how critical it is to start a project out in the right way.

SENSITIVITY TO INITIAL CONDITIONS

Initiating is the most important of the five stages of the project management process. At the initial stage, even a little misunderstanding about the project can bring disaster down the road. This principle is known as "sensitivity to initial conditions." If you start even one degree off course on a flight from Sydney to London, you might end up in Rio instead. The same is true with a project you're managing. Without a clear and shared picture of the outcome, the project is doomed.

Let's look at how this principle might play out in your world. Imagine that you have been put in charge of a company retreat. You've attended several retreats in the past, and secretly you have felt that if you had been in charge, things could have gone just a little bit better. So when your manager asked you to be in charge, you were excited about the opportunity. Traditionally the retreats have lasted three days, with the same basic agenda at each retreat. They've been held at the same location about thirty minutes from the office. Your manager is confident in your ability and sends you off with well wishes—advising you to use the past precedents as your guide. This will be a snap, you think. Ideas are already coming to mind as you begin to design the perfect event.

To make it more exciting, you determine a new location, hire two speakers you think fit the chosen profile and topic, and brainstorm a couple of instructional, fun team-building activities to add to the previous (boring) retreat agenda. You're excited about the results and look forward to hearing the praise from your colleagues and manager when the retreat reenergizes and reengages people and offers solutions to old challenges.

Several weeks later, following the busiest time of the year, you finally find time to meet with your manager to discuss the upcoming retreat, which is scheduled for early next week. You hand him the agenda and immediately realize something is wrong when he says, "No, no, no. That's not what we need to accomplish." He looks up at you and shakes his head. "We have to create an extensive launch plan for three new products. We don't have time for speakers or team-building. I'm not sure we'll make it even if we put our heads down and work the entire time."

You are crestfallen and apologetic, and you agree to make the adjustments necessary to meet his priorities. "And by the way," he concludes, "I hope this new location didn't cost a lot of money. It's a nice place, but given what we have to do this weekend, we could have just as easily stayed back at the office." Your heart sinks as you realize how much money and time you have wasted focusing on your ideas, not his. You realize now that you did not take the time to clarify what he wanted in the first place. Now, instead of receiving accolades, you might be looking for a new job.

Here is another example, not imaginary but real, and in our experience not an unusual situation. A project management consultant was called in to help on a multimillion-dollar project that was flopping badly. When he looked into it, he found nothing but fog: "My first job was to find out why all the stakeholders seemed to be on different planets, let alone different pages. So, I quizzed ten key stakeholders about a few key questions of the project ... It suffices to say that no two answers matched!"

These examples illustrate a root cause of project failure: a lack of shared expectations. According to experts, the primary reason for dismal project performance is "unrealistic expectations based on insufficient data and information."[2]

In other words, projects fail because nobody's clear about what to do. It won't matter if you work hard and finish the project on time and on budget. If the outcome isn't "right" in the eyes of the stakeholders, you've failed.

As a project leader, one of your most important jobs is to get everyone on the same page. This means that you are clarifying expectations for the project from the outset. This is not easy, and failing to do so is the biggest potential pitfall you can face as a project leader. Lacking a clear, shared set of expectations, you could end up doing the wrong project. Or you could go way off the budget. Or you could miss the deadline. Or everything at once! Sound familiar? As a project leader, you've got to make sure everybody sees the same picture of the outcome going forward.

So how do you make that happen? How do you make sure that the picture of the company retreat I have in my head matches the picture in your head? How do you create a shared understanding of the project outcomes?

You start by learning what everyone's expectations are. This is key. You may think everyone has the same thing in mind (e.g., "retreat" means a retreat like last year's), but a smart project leader starts with the assumption that nothing is clear. If you do that, you will avoid much pain down the road, pain that sounds like, "This isn't at all what we wanted or expected."

To get to a clear set of expectations, you must successfully answer these questions every time:

- Who will this project impact?
- Who determines success and what are their expectations?

- What are the project limitations?
- How do you create a shared understanding of the project outcomes?

To be able to answer these questions every time, we must follow these steps:

1. Identify all stakeholders.
2. Identify the key stakeholders.
3. Effectively interview the key stakeholders.

THE STAKEHOLDERS

You may have heard the term "stakeholder." In terms of a project, this is how we define one:

A STAKEHOLDER: *A person or an organization that is actively involved in the project or is positively or negatively impacted by it.*

Identify All Stakeholders

TOOL: GROUP BRAINSTORMING

Identify your stakeholders by brainstorming a list of all the people involved in or impacted by your project. Find a friend, coworker, member of your family, or member of your project team to help you with this. Brainstorming with a partner, particularly a work colleague, is a great project management tool for two reasons:

1. When you brainstorm, you invite your team or
    potential teammates to have a voice. When you
    ask them to participate in thinking through
    the project priorities, they feel respected and
    needed. It shows you care about their opinion.
    Involving them from the first will inspire them
    to want to play on your team!

2. Neuroscience shows that linear thinking is good,
    but brainstorming is better. Do random thinking,
    use Post-it Notes, or make thought maps. Include
    other people in your brainstorming. Creating a
    list of stakeholders by yourself is fine, but almost
    100 percent of the time, you will forget someone.
    And it could be someone extremely important.
    When you include other people in your list mak-
    ing, they will definitely think of stakeholders you
    would have missed on your own.

A major key to project management is to *never get blind-sided*. The more effort you spend identifying every possible person who might be "touched" by the project, the smaller the chance of failure. Have you ever worked on a project for a big chunk of time, only to have someone come to you very late and say, "Excuse me, but I just found out you are work-ing on this project. You can't move forward without my input and approval." Suddenly the project is off track because you inadvertently left out someone whose influence has a huge impact on the project's success. By taking the time to identify the entire universe of people who might be affected by your project, you will mitigate the risk of this potential mess-up right up front. And it will allow you to accurately identify the key stakeholders, the approvers, the signers, and more.

Let's look at the difference between a stakeholder and a key stakeholder.

Identify the Key Stakeholders

Project success is in the eye of the beholder. Or, in this case, in the eye of the key stakeholders. It stands to reason that the more key stakeholders give input to your project, the better your chance of success.

Who is a key stakeholder?

A KEY STAKEHOLDER: *Any person who determines the success or failure of the project.*

Most project leaders underestimate the importance of this step. They talk to only one client, one sponsor, or one manager, and then they think they have a clear picture of what is expected. "This is what Sally wants, so let's go get it done." But in this complex world of multiple, often competing priorities, no project has just one stakeholder. Many, many people are affected by what you do as a project leader—the list could include the project sponsor, the sponsor's boss, the sponsor's boss's boss, the finance lead (most crucially!), key department heads, and so on.

TOOL: KEY STAKEHOLDER D.A.N.C.E.

To mine your list of stakeholders to determine which stakeholders are key, use the following thinking tool with the acronym D.A.N.C.E. We call this tool the "Key Stakeholder Dance."

	RISK
DECISIONS	Make the decisions that control or influence the project budget.
AUTHORITY	Have the authority to grant permission to proceed with the project.
NEED	Directly benefit from or are impacted by the project and consequently need to know all about it.
CONNECTIONS	Are connected to the people, money, or resources required to remove roadblocks or exert influence to ensure project success.
ENERGY	Have positive or negative energy that could affect project success.

It's usually easy to identify those in the D, A, and N categories—the people who make the decisions, have the authority to grant permission, or benefit from the project. They tend to sign the budget or approve project outcomes. Be sure to identify every single one of them to avoid getting blindsided when you miss one.

In contrast, we find that very few project managers consider the C and E key stakeholders—the ones with the connections and energy that greatly influence the project's outcome. C stakeholders often have a substantial, but not initially obvious, impact on the project's success. People with connections may not be signers or approvers, but they are certainly high influencers. They have "skin in the game" because eventually they will be touched by or benefit from the outcome of your project. When possible, keep influencers involved throughout the project because they provide leverage on key stakeholders or the company in general. Because of their ability to persuade others, people with connections may be valuable at the key stakeholder table.

Now let's consider the E stakeholders—the ones with enough positive or negative energy to influence the project. Have you ever run across someone who just brings an air of negativity to most conversations? In some cases, it's simply their style or personality. You often wish they would go away, but they don't. This is where hidden agendas and politics can come into play. You cannot ignore these people; you must "lead" them. The Four Foundational Behaviors will help you with difficult personalities. If you respect and value the perspective they bring, listen empathically to their input, clarify their expectations, and are accountable for your commitments, then you will find that some of their negativity dissipates. Lean on other key stakeholders who might help you neutralize their negativity. Also clearly identify and involve any stakeholders with good, positive energy. With their help, you will fight fewer battles alone, leaving you to concentrate more on involving less energetic stakeholders.

Effectively Interview the Key Stakeholders

Once you have a complete list of key stakeholders, you'll want to get as much input from them as you can, as early as you can. Interview them thoroughly, and listen. The principle here is "frontloading," a term borrowed from the world of quality management. Frontloading means getting information totally clear up front. It means getting as much input as possible, as early as possible. It means listening before speaking, and listening hard—don't interrupt, just listen. Then do not be afraid to ask questions until you are as clear as possible about what is expected. The more information you start with, the less uncertainty you'll experience down the road.

Stop and think for a moment. When you currently launch a project, do you formally interview your key stakeholders? When we ask this question in our project management programs, only about 25 percent of participants say "yes." When we ask the remaining participants "Why not?" the answers are almost always the same:

- "I don't have, or I don't feel like I have, access to my key stakeholders."
- "I don't want the stakeholders to lose confidence in me. Doesn't asking questions make me look dumb?"
- "I've never been taught interviewing skills."
- "I didn't know I was supposed to interview them."
- "I think I already know what they want."

With just a little preparation, you can access your key stakeholders and be seen as highly credible. When you schedule interviews with them, let them know the purpose of your time together and what you are trying to accomplish. Everyone, especially stakeholders whose time is limited, needs to know WIIFM ("What's in it for me?"). They must know the value of the interview before they take time out of their busy schedules to answer your questions. So be sure to include some of the benefits of the interview when you ask for their time. Include things like:

- "I know this project means a lot to our organizational goals, so I want to make sure I have all the information I need from you to make it a great success."

- "I want to make sure I completely understand your expectations to ensure great success on the project outcome."

- "You play an integral part in the success of this project."

"But I can never get access to these busy key stakeholders," you're saying. "They barely even know I exist, let alone know the role I'm playing on the project." But they aren't trying to sabotage your project by being vague or unavailable. They're just busy. And because they're busy, you need the courage to step up, let the key stakeholder know the value of the time you're asking for, and be prepared with a few key questions to help guide the conversation. They will appreciate it more often than not.

To be a great interviewer, you just need to be well prepared. Know what you want to get out of the short time you will have with the key stakeholder, prepare a few good questions, and wear a very big pair of ears to listen deeply.

If you think you "already know what they want," you're indulging in some pretty risky thinking. Here's a simple illustration.

Let's say there is a member of my team named Liam. He is someone I like as a person, but he's not always the best project team member.

One day Liam sticks his head in my office on his way to lunch and asks if I would like him to bring me anything.

"How nice of you to ask," I say. "Would you mind bringing me an apple?"

"Sure, no problem!" He pulls on his coat as he walks out the door.

I grab my computer and walk down the hall to a meeting.

When I get back, there is an apple sitting on my desk. I shake my head sadly and think, *I appreciate the offer, but this isn't what I wanted.*

So what went wrong?

Neither of us grasped a critical principle of project management: *Words are only code for the pictures in our minds.*

So what was the picture in my mind of the apple? It was a big, juicy Red Delicious apple. Instead, I saw on my desk a small, unripe, green apple. I deeply dislike green apples!

Liam assumed what I wanted without asking. I assumed he understood that good apples are large, not small, and red, not green. In truth, we let each other down.

If one or both of us had clarified the picture in our minds, Liam would have very likely come back with the type of apple I wanted. Our conversation might have gone something like this:

> LIAM: "Kory, can I get you anything when I go out for lunch?"
>
> KORY: "How nice of you to ask. Would you mind bringing me an apple?"
>
> LIAM: "In order to get you what you expect, and since there are a lot of apple types, what size and color and type do you prefer?"
>
> KORY: "Liam, thank you so much for clarifying. I'd like something medium to large, and it must be red. In fact, a Red Delicious would be perfect."
>
> LIAM: "So, if they only have green?"
>
> KORY: "It would be a waste of money because I really don't like them. Thanks for checking with me."
>
> LIAM: "No problem."

Now Liam has the same picture in his head that I have in mine. Expectations are clear. While the story is simple, the principle behind it has significant application to every project.

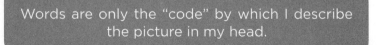

Words are only the "code" by which I describe the picture in my head.

The goal in your interviews with key stakeholders is to decipher or decode the pictures in their minds. Think back to the retreat you were asked to organize. If the manager had told you, "Come up with a quality way to spend our time," would you *assume* you knew what "quality" means? If so, you'd go off and plan the project only to find that

> initiate

"quality" to you meant something completely different to him. When you don't get the picture exactly right, you end up with disappointment and failure.

Your goal is to understand the unique perspectives and desired results of each key stakeholder before you begin the project.

TOOL: KEY STAKEHOLDER INTERVIEW

Use the Key Stakeholder Interview tool on the next page and you'll see how easy it will be to decipher the right picture every time.

Let's look briefly at each part of this key tool, using the retreat-planning example from earlier in this chapter:

Project Purpose. The Project Purpose statement describes why you are doing the project in the first place. It answers the question "How does this project affect the goals of the department or organization?" Hindsight being 20/20, you now know that the purpose of your retreat was to provide a venue for the team to do uninterrupted work on the sales plan. (Note that the tool contains a line item for the Project Purpose and another for Desired Results. What is the difference between the two?)

Description. In this space you answer the how, the what, and the when of the project as clearly as possible. Go into detail here. "Is the retreat a four-hour session or all day? Near the office or at some destination resort? Is the date firm? How will participants get there?" And so forth.

Desired Results. The Desired Results statement defines project success. It answers this question: "What are the

KEY STAKEHOLDER INTERVIEW

Interviewee: Date:

Interviewer:

PROJECT PURPOSE (key reason[s] for the project)

DESCRIPTION (the how, what, and when of key deliverables)

DESIRED RESULTS (a prioritized list of specific and measurable deliverables)

EXCLUSIONS (items out of scope)

COMMUNICATION NEEDS (who, how, and how often)

Interviewee: How often:

ACCEPTANCE CRITERIA (who needs to sign off on what, and how they will sign off)

CONSTRAINTS (a prioritized list of restrictions or limitations)

1.   4.

2.   5.

3.   6.

specific measures and outcomes that must be accomplished?" Originally, you planned the retreat on the assumption that the desired result was happy, united, well-rested colleagues. But this wasn't the boss's definition of success. Instead, the desired result was three well-defined launch plans for new products, which you would have known if you had thought this tool through with the boss.

Exclusions. These are considerations or elements that will *not* be part of the project. For example, it would have been helpful to know that you shouldn't even consider an off-site location for this year's retreat. Imagine how knowing this exclusion up front would have mitigated the notorious scope creep and saved you time, money, and headaches.

Communication Needs. A huge factor in project success is good communication. Ask stakeholders, "What do you need to know as the project proceeds? How would you like us to communicate with you?" Everyone wants information differently in our age: email, text, teleconferences, Skype. Time zone differences come into play as well. So get clear with key stakeholders on specifically what they want to know and how. You don't want miscommunication when you are deep into the project and can least afford it.

Acceptance Criteria. Here you decide who needs to sign off on the project. Have you ever had to stop a project because you "forgot" to get the approval of someone influential? Use this tool to decide who the ultimate decision makers are and get their sign-off.

Constraints. These are restrictions or limitations on the project, and they generally fall into six areas identified by the PMI, as the Areas of Possible Constraints illustration on the next page shows.

Areas of Possible Constraints

SCOPE
The sum of the products, services, and results to be provided.

QUALITY
The degree to which project characteristics fulfill requirements.

RESOURCES
People (individuals or teams), equipment, services, or supplies needed to fulfill requirements.

BUDGET
The approved estimate for the project.

RISK
An uncertain event or condition that, if it occurs, has an effect (usually negative) on project results.

TIME
The deadlines by which products, services, and results are to be delivered.

Constraints are like threads in a spider's web. If you pull on one, the rest of them are affected, too. It is your responsibility as a project manager to recognize the constraints on a project and then ask your key stakeholders to determine which have the highest priority.

One of our colleagues, Shelly, tells this story:

I was walking down the hall one day when the CEO stopped me. "I've been looking for you," he said. "I've got a quick project, and I need your help."

As the CEO continued talking, I learned he was heading to a trade show to market our product to a new demographic.

He continued: "Here is what I need from you: one high-quality brochure with the right messaging for this new market. I think we need about a thousand of them by next Thursday when I board the plane."

I replied, "Okay. So how much do we have to spend on this project, and who can help me?"

"I was only planning around five hundred dollars," he responded. "And I really don't think we have any people to spare. But it ought to be a very simple project."

Before I learned project management skills, I would have taken this information, walked back to my desk, and promptly pulled my hair out. Instead, I asked the CEO to help me prioritize the list of constraints. I reframed his expectations, "Which item is most important: a high-quality brochure, the new messaging, having a thousand completed brochures by Thursday, et cetera?"

He answered with a typical CEO response: "All of them!"

I paused, counted to ten, and then asked the question a different way. "I know they are all important, but let's put it this way. Is having a marketing piece at the trade show the most important thing? Could we collect business cards and send the marketing piece to them later?"

He thought for a minute. "No," he said, "I don't think it will have as much impact. I need to have a piece with me there."

"Okay, so would you say having a piece by Thursday is our most important priority?" I reiterated.

"Yes."

"Great, that is really helpful." I continued, "So does it have to be a really high-quality piece with on-point messaging and customized photos, or would you be willing to settle for something a little more generic?"

He paused to think again. "No, it has to be high quality. This is a new market for us. I want to make a great impression. I want them to look at this piece and immediately know that we understand the market, and that we know what we are talking about. Besides, I've spent ten thousand on this event already. I don't want to go cheap now."

"I get it," I said. "And it makes a lot of sense. So we need a high-quality brochure by Thursday."

He adamantly nodded his head.

"Okay, I think I can make this happen, but only if I have a team of people and a budget bigger than five hundred dollars. Without that, I can say yes to you right now, but I can't promise I can deliver exactly what you want. You have identified that Thursday and quality are your highest priorities."

He nodded again.

"If that's the case, can you help me with people resources and a bigger budget so I can ensure I get you what you really need?" I asked unapologetically.

"How much and who?" he responded.

"I can let you know that very quickly if you give me a little time to plan," I said.

"Okay, do that and get back to me. I'll move some things in the budget and talk to some of the department heads about people that can help you."

I smiled as I walked away.

Why did Shelly smile? Because by clarifying expectations and prioritizing the list of constraints, she was able to negotiate a larger budget and more resources. Instead of pulling her hair out, she created a far better chance of meeting the desired results. Of course it won't be easy— the deadline is tight, and there is a lot of work to do—but because of this conversation, at least she has a *chance* at a successful outcome.

> initiate

Try This at Home

Think about the principles of the constraint model when you're doing day-to-day time and life management. Taking the time to consciously filter the possible barriers with a process like this up front for the family reunion or even a picnic can reduce your stress level dramatically. And, as your personal project starts to morph and change (maybe because of those family key stakeholders!), you use the constraint model to continually uncover the possible barriers that you may not have seen coming otherwise.

By now you no doubt understand why it's so important to conduct key stakeholder interviews. The more information you get from key stakeholders, the clearer the expectations will be for meeting the project's desired outcomes.

The better the discussion about constraints with key stakeholders, the clearer the expectations become for meeting the desired outcome of the project!

TOOL: QUESTION FUNNEL

To get more precise information in the key stakeholder interview, we use a tool called the "Question Funnel." It helps you go from generic to specific information in your interview, and to get as close as possible to the pictures in your key stakeholders' minds.

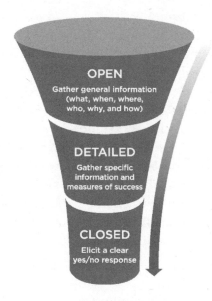

To get the right answers, you need to ask the right questions. There are three types of questions to ask to get to the concrete and clear answers you must have.

1. **Open** questions get at the broad, big picture: "How do you define success on this project"?

2. **Detailed** questions drill down to "leaner" information: "Could you tell me more about what that means to you or what it would look like"?

› initiate

3. **Closed** questions are the key to success in the interview: "So here is what I heard you say . . . did I get that exactly right?" Use the closed questions to validate that you really understand the pictures your interviewees have in their minds. Make sure there are no unclear assumptions left on the table.

Prepare a few questions for each stakeholder that will yield the answers you seek. Don't get so hung up on your list that you don't hear the answers. Make sure you listen carefully to the answers and digest them. If you don't hear what you are listening for, or if the answer is too general (remember the story of the green and red apples?), ask again! As long as you keep the end in mind (to decode stakeholders' mental pictures of success), you will prepare the right questions that will lead you to the right answers.

Don't be surprised if your questions change the initial trajectory of the project. Grateful key stakeholders tell us all the time that good interviews can shed a whole new light on a project. They report often seeing project outcomes very differently as a result of the interview—and they even change their position or opinion on how the project should proceed. Because their project managers have learned these interviewing skills, they are asking more and better questions than ever before.

THE GROUP INTERVIEW

Let's demonstrate the Project Purpose from our Key Stakeholder Interview tool. The question is, "What does success look like for you on this project?"

The answer you want is *not* a vague response like this: "We are doing this because senior leadership says it's important." Instead, you want something specific like this: "The project supports our strategy to increase market share by 20 percent."

It's not that the first answer is wrong; it's simply not precise enough and is full of unspoken assumptions. Remember, words are code for an internal picture; to clearly see the image in the stakeholder's head, you need clear, measurable answers. You likely will have to ask follow-up questions to their vague responses: "Why does senior leadership think it's important? What goal or strategy does this project connect to?" Such follow-up questions will quickly lead the stakeholder to a more concrete and specific response. The clearer and more measurable the outcome, the higher probability of getting key stakeholders on the same page.

Because everyone is busy, we often get asked if the interviewing process can be simplified. The answer is yes, but be careful! Key stakeholder interviews can be done one-on-one or in a group. However, we strongly recommend one-on-one so you get the individual stakeholder's concentration and best thinking.

That said, we know it is not always possible to do individual interviews. There are advantages and disadvantages to both one-on-one and group interviews.

One-on-one interviews. The good thing about getting together person to person is that you can find out what's really on the stakeholder's mind. They're more likely to open up in private and give you a better idea of what they expect from the project. The downside is that you lose the natural synergy of a good group discussion. Interviewing people one by one can also use up a lot of time.

Group interviews. The good thing about group interviews is you receive a lot more input faster than if you interview individuals. And if you do the group interview right, it may give you better insights than you could have gotten from any one individual. That's called "synergy." But a group interview can go wrong. With everyone trying to talk at once and take over the agenda, it can turn into a pointless free-for-all.

Here's how to conduct a group interview:

- Get as many stakeholders as you can together in one room or online.

- Set a strict time limit. Promise to stop the meeting at the set time, and keep your promise.

- Set a ground rule that no one can interrupt anyone else. The purpose of *this* session is for every stakeholder to hear out every other stakeholder.

- Give each person only a few minutes to answer your questions.

- Don't argue with any of the points raised. Ask a question only if you need clarification. Then thank the contributor and move on.

- Carefully record everyone's comments.
- Thank the group and invite them to speak to you one-on-one if they have more issues to raise.
- Distribute the record to everyone after the meeting.

It's also a good idea to post the Four Foundational Behaviors as ground rules and explain that this is how you work:

- Demonstrate respect.
- Listen first.
- Clarify expectations.
- Practice accountability.

Something to keep in mind: Projects attract controversy. Stakeholders will question each other, the approach you're taking, the details of the project, costs, resources, timing— even the value of doing the project at all. All of this can be a very rich discussion as long as you are leading it effectively. That's why your Foundational Behaviors are so important to this meeting.

Explain that they are here to listen respectfully to everyone else and that your purpose is to be very clear on their expectations of the project. Explain that you will hold yourself *and them* accountable for those expectations.

If you start your project with this rich, robust download, based on ground rules of respect and understanding, your informal authority will skyrocket.

THE SCOPE OF THE PROJECT

So where is all of this hard work leading? To a beautiful Project Scope Statement: one clear set of expectations approved by all of the key stakeholders. A standard project management tool, the scope statement is so called because it describes the scope of the project or the "borders" around the project.

The *Project Management Body of Knowledge* (PMBOK) defines the scope statement like this: "The scope statement provides a documented basis for making future project decisions and for confirming or developing common understanding of project scope among the stakeholders. As the project progresses, the scope statement may need to be revised or refined to reflect approved changes to the scope of the project."[3]

At this stage of project planning, as Stephen R. Covey said in his bestselling book *The 7 Habits of Highly Effective People*, "We are more in need of a compass than a road map. We often don't know what the terrain ahead will be like or what we will need to go through it; much will depend on our judgment at the time. But a compass will always give us direction."[4]

The scope statement is your compass for the project. It tells you in which direction to go. It has many benefits: Stakeholders can see in one place the why, what, when, and how of the project. It gives you the guidance you need for deciding what to do and what not to do. It describes clearly what success looks like.

Maybe best of all, the scope statement carries the signatures of key stakeholders. It represents all views and a consensus. Once they have signed off on the scope statement, you have at least some leverage for holding them accountable for their decisions. This leverage can be very helpful to an unofficial project manager, especially if people start to change their minds about the project scope. In a nutshell, *a scope statement gets the key stakeholders all on the same page with a crystal-clear end in mind for project success.*

Creating an Approved Project Scope Statement

There are three steps to developing the Project Scope Statement:

1. Draft a scope statement.
2. Review the statement.
3. Get approvals.

Seth Godin says, "During the magical early stages of the project, we envision not just perfect execution, but limitless features. At this stage, every project needs a truth teller ... not a no-sayer, because they are easy to find and worthless."[5] As project manager, you need to be the truth teller: Tell the truth about what this project is all about, what its limitations are, where it's heading, and so forth. If you did a good job in the key stakeholder interviews, particularly around Exclusion and Constraint priorities, there's less risk that your project will become someone's "wish list." Instead, key stakeholders will have a shared and concrete vision of the project.

TOOL: PROJECT SCOPE STATEMENT

The Project Scope Statement has the same line items as your Key Stakeholder Interview tool. You combine all of the information gleaned from your interviews to form a clear picture of the scope of the project. Your tool for creating the scope statement is on the next page.

All About Eve

Eve was a busy nurse in a medium-sized hospital in Brazil. Recently, she'd been promoted to take charge of in-house training, but one day she went back on the floor to fill in for a nurse on vacation.

As soon as she started her rounds that day, she knew something was wrong. Two patients were far worse than they had been the night before. One, a teenager named Luiza, reminded Eve of her little sister. Eve had quickly formed a bond with Luiza while she recovered from pneumonia. Now, Luiza was doubled over and convulsing with pain and a high fever. By noon, two more patients in the same ward had gotten sicker, and Luiza was near death.

Eve worked with the medical team all night fighting Luiza's rampaging infection with antibiotics, and they got it under control by morning. Exhausted, Eve knew the problem was infection by *Clostridium difficile* (*C. diff*), a potentially deadly bacterium that sporadically hit her patients.

PROJECT SCOPE STATEMENT

Project Name: Projected start:

Completed by: Projected duration:

PROJECT PURPOSE:

PROJECT DESCRIPTION:

DESIRED RESULTS:

EXCLUSIONS:

COMMUNICATION NEEDS:

ACCEPTANCE CRITERIA:

CONSTRAINTS:

APPROVALS:

Not again, Eve thought. She'd been battling hospital-acquired infections (HAIs) for years. She'd seen too many people get sicker inside the hospital than they'd been before they came. Watching it happen to Luiza made Eve more frustrated than ever before.

"We need to do something about this," she told the head of nursing the next day. "We can't just live with HAIs forever. Eventually, someone is going to die. Before that happens, we need to find a solution."

"It's a problem everywhere," the head nurse sighed. "We're no worse off than any other hospital."

"No better, either. We need to do something," Eve repeated. She couldn't get her sick patients out of her mind.

The head nurse agreed. Together, she and Eve met with Senta, the hospital administrator, who asked Eve if she had any ideas on how to cut back on HAIs. Well, she had a few. "Good," said the administrator. "Would you be willing to lead up a project?"

Before she had time to think about it, Eve was a project manager. She'd never led a project like this before and slept restlessly that night. She didn't have to do this. Her job was consuming enough—training, testing, monitoring nurses around the clock—and she knew there wouldn't be any letup in that part of her job. Still, she was committed.

With the help of her colleagues, she brainstormed her list of stakeholders. From this list she determined the key stakeholders: the hospital administrator, two particular doctors with heavy experience in this area, and a consultant in infectious diseases. She also included a board member, the marketing director, and the financial analyst.

Eve conducted a few one-on-one interviews and decided to hold a group interview with everyone else. She found a date when everyone could meet. After explaining the ground rules, she started to ask her questions: "How do you see the problem? What is it costing us? What's causing the problem? What do you think we should do about it? What would be a reasonable goal? Who should be on the project team?"

Things went well until it was the turn of Dr. Saltas. One of the top surgeons, he was famous for speaking his mind and annoying people in the process. "I don't know why we spend any time on this. Our HAI rate is within acceptable limits. These are random outbreaks, and you're never going to eliminate randomness from any system, so why waste our time?"

Eve bristled. She'd always tried to avoid Dr. Saltas because his ego filled any room he was in. Instead of thinking of the patients, it seemed he could only focus on randomness, systems, and acceptable limits. But she respected the rule of the Four Foundational Behaviors and said, "Thank you, Doctor. Next?" and turned to the next person on the list.

Eve hadn't realized the whole issue had touched some nerves. Taking their cue from Dr. Saltas, the other doctors got defensive. One spoke up, saying she was tired of being blamed for a problem beyond her control; she was already doing everything she could think of to protect her patients. The infectious diseases consultant was skeptical about changing the HAI rate, since his research showed it really was an intractable problem. After each person spoke, Eve moved to the next stakeholder.

Finally, Eve took the floor. "Look, I know HAIs happen everywhere. I know our infection rate is within acceptable limits, but I also believe we can do better. I didn't become a nurse because I feel okay about making people sicker. I watched my mother battle cancer for years. The nurses and doctors became my family. I trusted and relied on them every step of the way. Of course we can just ignore this, but maybe we can do something about it, too. Isn't that the reason we got into medicine—to be a hero to our patients? To actually fix what is broken?"

After that, the room was quiet. Then the aged, unruffled Dr. Leron, the head of the medical staff, congratulated Eve on her work with all of the key stakeholders. "Eve has a very good point. If something more can be done about HAIs, we should do it." His voice was calm but firm. "I propose this hospital formally seek a solution." Nothing else needed to be said; Eve had her charter for the project.

Eve learned a lot in this meeting, but so did the key stakeholders. Most didn't know that the HAI rate was growing. The financial analyst shared the terrible monetary cost of treating these infections, the lawyer warned about the risk of lawsuits if someone died, and the head of nursing talked about the danger to the patient population. The doctors were defensive, but because of the ground rules, they could get most of their concerns off their chests without sparking a big argument.

Most important, with a little help from Eve, the team remembered why doing something about the infections was so important.

By the end of the meeting, nearly everyone saw that HAIs were a big problem worth solving. Eve had enough information to begin to draft a scope statement. It looked like this:

PROJECT SCOPE STATEMENT

Project Name: Hospital-Acquired Infections Reduction   Projected start: 11 October

Completed by. Eve Berg   Projected end. 12 October

PROJECT PURPOSE

To find out what is causing HAIs

DESCRIPTION

We will create a comprehensive system for preventing infectious agents from entering the facility and from migrating through the facility.

DESIRED RESULTS

To reduce hospital-acquired infections (HAIs) from 9% of the patients to 4%. Each HAI costs the hospital $12,500.

EXCLUSIONS

We will only focus on the main location and will decide to proceed with a reduction at sister locations when this project is complete.

COMMUNICATION NEEDS

Weekly update meeting to key stakeholders

ACCEPTANCE CRITERIA

Legal sign off by 10/13
Budget Approval by 10/16

CONSTRAINTS

1. Budget: $37,000 estimated, plan forthcoming

2. Team members: Dr. Leron, Senta, Dr. Saltas, Consultant, Legal, Head of Nursing

3.

4. Technology: current equipment is sufficient for analysis purposes

5.

6.

APPROVALS

KEY STAKEHOLDERS	INTERVIEW DATE	APPROVAL
Dr. Saltas		
Finance Department		
Head Nurse Smalley		
Dr. Leron		
Senta		
Hospital Administrator		

Eve distributed the scope statement draft to all stakeholders. It got people talking, sharing ideas, and making suggestions. A few things changed, but the scope of the project remained the same, and a few days later the key stakeholders all signed the second draft. Even the touchy Dr. Saltas agreed that the goal was reasonable. Eve's project was under way.

Imagine what would have happened if Eve hadn't followed the simple steps of this initiating process. Her only authority would be an offhand verbal agreement with a hospital administrator. She'd be getting little or no support from a lot of busy people, all with priorities of their own. She wouldn't know if the project could be made profitable or how much budget she needed. She wouldn't even know exactly what the goal was—to stop all infections? Half of them? At what cost?

Can you see her asking the hospital board for $37,000 for a project without a clear goal?

Furthermore, anything she suggested would require some people to change their behavior. Somebody was responsible for spreading infection— maybe a lot of somebodies. If you've ever tried changing your own behavior, can you guess how hard it is to change somebody else's?

Can you see her a few months from now trying to enforce a set of guidelines that busy, professional doctors and nurses didn't know about and had no input on?

Can you see her making no difference at all by the end of the next year?

"There is nothing more difficult to take in hand, more perilous to conduct, or more uncertain in its success, than to take the lead in introducing a new order of things."
—NICCOLÒ MACHIAVELLI

Like a blindfolded person trying to walk a straight line, she would most likely end up circling right back where she started.

But by following the initiating process, Eve has the equivalent of a compass that shows her which direction to go. The scope statement provides clear, *shared* expectations for the project. There are no guarantees in project work, but now Eve's chances of getting it right have gone way up.

TO SUM UP ⋒

INITIATE Skillset and Toolset

➤ **Skill:** Identify All Stakeholders
   Tool: Group Brainstorming

➤ **Skill:** Identify Key Stakeholders
   Tool: Key Stakeholder D.A.N.C.E.

➤ **Skill:** Interview Key Stakeholders
   Tool: Key Stakeholder Interview
   Tool: Question Funnel

➤ **Skill:** Document Project Scope Statement
   Tool: Project Scope Statement

Initiating the project is the most important phase because everything else depends on it. If you don't initiate right, nothing will ever be right. You'll be climbing a ladder that's leaning against the wrong wall.

To initiate a project is to first make sure you have identified every possible stakeholder that could be touched by the project, so you can never be blindsided. Next, identify all the obvious and not-so-obvious key stakeholders. If this is done well, then you are in a position to pinpoint the purpose, description, and constraints of the project accurately; in other words, questions like "Why are we doing this?" "What will it look like?" and "How much time and money do we have to get it done?" These things define the scope of the project.

There's a right way and wrong way to initiate a project. The right way is to invest the time to frontload the project. The return on this investment is vast. If you do not frontload as we've described, you'll end up doing a whole lot of "backloading"—tearing your work up and starting over again and again until the time and money runs out and you can't deliver.

Frontloading is the basic principle of project success. Only a fool would try a project like climbing Mount Everest without careful frontloading. Before climbing Mount Everest, you'd frontload like crazy; you'd research it and talk to the best people you could find. You'd scope out all the constraints—time, cost, equipment, and team. You'd check and double-check all your assumptions. This is what you are doing when you identify the stakeholders, interview them, and develop a Project Scope Statement. The better you initiate a project in this way, the better your chance of success.

CHECK YOUR LEARNING—
INITIATING THE PROJECT

✓ Do I know who this project will impact?

✓ Do I know who determines success?

✓ Have I clarified expectations?

✓ Do I know the project's constraints or limitations?

✓ Have I created a shared understanding of the project's outcomes?

CHAPTER 4

Planning the Project: Milestone or Mirage?

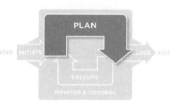

PLAN Mindset:
You must create a clear road map for smart decision making.

O LIVIA WAS A BUSY DIRECTOR of operations in a medium-sized company in the southwestern United States. In a special management meeting, her CEO announced that the company was going to relocate within the year to a city hundreds of miles away. The current headquarters was in a small marketplace that no longer met the needs of the growing company. The local talent pool wasn't big enough to get the good hires they wanted. Plus, given an increasing number of international customers, travel was getting too expensive. The new location would allow faster, cheaper access to their global customers and access to a better talent pool.

The CEO asked Olivia, who was responsible for running the business day to day, to take charge of relocating the staff and recruiting new employees in the new location. He also asked her to train all new employees to be ready to go as soon as the doors opened in the new city. She was to do all this *and* make sure the business operations and the quality of customer service didn't suffer at all during the transition. Wow. Though Olivia was well known for high output and quality work, she realized that for the first time, she would have to get serious about project management.

Like all projects, this one was fraught with constraints. Could she do the project on time and with quality? Could she keep control of the scope? Would she have enough resources to fulfill the requirements? And what about the risks?

As Olivia thought about her new project, her eyes got wider and wider. She knew it would either ruin her reputation or make her a hero. The success of the relocation was now resting squarely on her shoulders. She was smart enough to know that she was the project's "key success (or failure) factor." So she went to work putting together a team, identifying and interviewing stakeholders, and creating a Project Scope Statement.

In **Initiate**, Olivia identified all of her project stakeholders and then figured out which would determine project success—these were her key stakeholders. She then interviewed them carefully, asking great questions and listening intently. She helped the CEO prioritize constraints, and she didn't stop until she was clear about everyone's expectations. Last, she delivered a detailed scope statement that was signed by all key stakeholders.

Now it was time to plan the project.

> Like a compass, the scope statement tells you what direction to go. Like a road map, the project plans tell you how to get there.

PLAN A RISK MANAGEMENT STRATEGY

Are you familiar with "Murphy"? We all run into him from time to time, especially when we least expect it. According to Murphy's Law, "Anything that can go wrong, will." It's much better to vigilantly plan for the inevitable "What ifs" instead of dealing with the pain of "If only." Naturally, some "What ifs" might occur, but you can keep them to a minimum by creating a risk management strategy.

Identify the Risks

First, identify the risks to the project and then assess their impact. Because the risk assessment will affect your planning, assess the impact of each risk before attempting to put together a project schedule.

To identify risks to the project, you'll essentially make a list of things that could go wrong. Here's a sample list of some of the things that could go wrong with Olivia's project.

- Not enough qualified job candidates in new location.

- Not enough budget to train new employees.

- Current compensation plans not high enough in new area for qualified staff.

- Housing not available for relocation.

- Not enough human resources/capacity to train new hires.

- Quality of customer service suffers during transition because new employees are in training.

Any or all of these risks, plus others, could affect Olivia's success. Financial resources, team strength, suppliers, technology, disruptive innovations, political issues—all of these are potential sources of risk to any project. Olivia brainstormed with her team as many risk factors as they could imagine. She wanted to make sure she put all the possible risks on the table to avoid getting blindsided later.

Assessing the risks soon started to feel a little overwhelming for Olivia. How was she ever going to manage all of them? How was she going to get the project and every other part of her job done while managing so many risk factors? And what if all of the risks actually became realities?

One evening, when Olivia was feeling overwhelmed, she shared her high stress with a trusted friend experienced in project management, who explained to her how to prioritize the risks. He told her there was no way she could properly manage all of the risks without paralyzing herself and the project. He suggested she "weigh" the risks with an easy calculation. As she did this, she realized that not all of them deserved equal thought and attention. By classifying risks as high, medium, or low, she felt less overwhelmed and better able to create a risk management plan.

Assess the Risks

Here's the formula for assessing each risk factor:

Impact x Probability = Actual Risk

What is the *impact* of each risk factor on the overall success of the project? How serious would the impact be? A 5 (worst-case scenario), a 4 (relatively important impact), or a 2 (minimal impact)?

And what is the *probability* of each risk factor? A 5 (a high likelihood it will happen), a 3 (a 50–50 chance it will happen), a 2 (it could happen), or a 1 (a slight possibility it could happen under unusual conditions)?

Once you have brainstormed all the possible risks, evaluate them for both impact and probability. Then multiply the resulting numbers to find the "actual risk" score. For risks that score 12 or higher, you will need to take the time to think through and identify a strategy to reduce the risk.

By doing this evaluation, you'll realize which risks absolutely need a plan and which ones are less likely to occur. In some cases, you can even plan to ensure that the risk remains low. Either way, like Olivia, with a plan you will feel less stress.

Olivia gave each risk factor an impact and probability score. Then she multiplied the scores for each factor.

>> plan

TOOL: RISK MATRIX

	RISK	IMPACT	PROBABILITY	SCORE
R4	Housing not available for relocated employees	4	3	12
R2	Compensation not high enough for new city	4	2	8
R3	Not enough qualified job candidates in new city	5	2	10
R5	Can't get training done	5	4	20
R1	Not enough budget to train new employees	5	1	5
R6	Customer service goes down	5	4	20

The housing challenge was a significant risk on Olivia's list. If a large number of the current employees transferred to the new city, a lack of housing would greatly impact the project's success—and she would fail to meet the project scope and key stakeholder expectations. On the other hand, if only a few employees made the move, she would have a larger number of new workers to train. Either way, these risks posed big problems. So she decided to rank both their impact and probability high and put a formal risk strategy into play. There was also a high risk that she wouldn't be able to complete their training and that customer service would drop, so these, too, needed formal risk management strategies. At the same time, she resolved to keep an eye on the low (score of 0–5) and medium (score of 6–10) risks to make sure they stayed below 12 and didn't overwhelm or paralyze her.

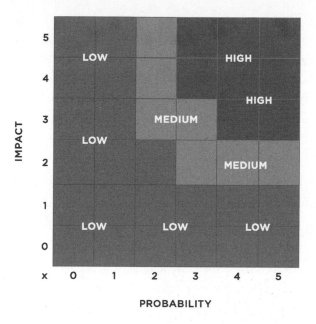

Tame the Risks

Tool: TAME the Risks

So, what did she do with the high-scoring risks? For the risks she rated at 12 or higher, she needed to TAME them. TAME is a thinking tool to help you filter through possible strategies to minimize risk. It gives you four options for managing risk (or more, if you combine options).

- **Transfer the risk:** Shift it to a third party.
- **Accept the risk:** Acknowledge it and deal with it if it occurs.
- **Mitigate the risk:** Reduce its probability or impact.
- **Eliminate the risk:** Do what you must to make it go away.

Try This at Home

Think about the principles of "risk management" when you're doing day-to-day time and life management. Just taking the time to consciously brainstorm a list of risks, identifying the highest ones *before* they happen and figuring out how to *keep* them from happening, can be life changing in all your personal planning.

Olivia thought through her options for TAMEing the housing risk. She determined she could *transfer* the risk if she contracted early with a relocation company, one that would know the area well and have contacts. As the one on the hook for getting everyone housed, she would have to carefully manage the progress of the relocation company toward her project deliverables.

Just *accepting* the risk was not an option. There was too much at stake to simply hope it would all work out.

She decided that she could also *mitigate* the risk of inadequate housing availability by reserving temporary hotel accommodations, which would lessen its impact. By ensuring she had a block of rooms available, she could offset the last-minute problems of people who did not have a place to stay.

As much as she wanted to make this risk completely disappear—to *eliminate* it—she knew it was not reality.

So she settled on *transferring* and *mitigating* the risk of inadequate housing. The relocation company would minimize most of the risk, and a block of hotel rooms would not adversely affect her budget if they weren't used. With both strategies in place, Olivia knew a potential lack of housing would no longer be a major problem.

Next she thought about the training-capacity risk. Since she wasn't sure yet who would move and who would stay, she couldn't determine her capacity for training. Since training was key to successful project completion, she decided that she would *transfer* some of the new employee training to a trusted learning and development firm. Having the firm on standby for the bulk of the training would free her to keep track of other important parts of the project.

Her last high risk was the prospect of a temporary lapse in customer service while new people were hired and trained. Olivia knew she could *mitigate* this risk by contracting with a temporary employment agency the company had used during the previous holiday season. Her contacts at this agency already knew her business and the type and experience of the people she would need, which would minimize the time needed to get them up to speed and maximize her ability to continue to offer great customer service.

Like Olivia, you won't be able to eliminate all risk. Still, you must think through all of the TAME options when building your risk management strategy. That's why it's so crucial to clarify expectations on the front end. If you've done your scoping work properly, you should have a strong sense of what's possible and what isn't.

Tool: Risk Management Plan

Now you have to communicate in a plan these risks and your strategies to address them.

RISK MANAGEMENT PLAN

Project Name:

Date:

Prepared by:

RISK	SCORE	STRATEGY	WHO

Once you've determined your risk strategy, document it in a risk management plan (shown on page 86) that can be easily communicated to key stakeholders and the team.

To be respectful and accountable to your stakeholders, be honest about the high-scoring risks. If the risk of failure is great, you have an obligation to communicate it to your stakeholders. And, of course, clarify the risk management plan with your team.

Communication is 90 percent of a project's success. By documenting the top risks and the plan to offset them, everyone on your team can row in the same direction. When you understand the potential pressures and challenges of risks, you and your team will pull together to TAME the risks and raise the probability of project success.

In summary, Olivia created a risk management plan to record each risk, its impact/probability score, a strategy for dealing with the risk, and the person on her team responsible for that strategy.

RISK	SCORE	STRATEGY	WHO
· R6- Housing not available	12	Temporary hotel blocks — Hire relocation company	Jill
· R7- Not enough training capacity	20	Hire consulting company	Olivia
· R8- Customer service goes down	20	Schedule specific employees from temp agency	Tai

What does your risk assessment strategy have to do with your planning? Action items from your risk management plan will now go into your overall project plan. In Olivia's case, she will own some of the activities and delegate others to the team.

CREATE A PROJECT SCHEDULE

Now that you've planned out how to manage risk, you can create the project schedule.

If you're managing a project, you've got to know what to do when. The schedule becomes the road map. That's why experienced project managers break projects down into bite-sized pieces and schedule each piece.

The schedule contains all the key tasks and milestones needed to complete the project. It tells you if you're on track or not, so it should be visible, constantly updated, and open to every team member. Otherwise, your project team is working in the dark. Imagine sports teams playing without a scoreboard—how could you tell if you were winning or not? So make sure the project schedule is always in view and up to date at all times.

The schedule contains all the key tasks and milestones needed to complete the project. To create the schedule, you can use project planning software or a spreadsheet program (like Excel) or just sketch it out on paper.

In an effort to manage projects better, many organizations invest in expensive, sophisticated project management software. Often they become so entranced with managing the project management *software*, they forget to manage the project. Others enthusiastically install and open the software, look at it for a few minutes, or even investigate it for a few hours. But after an initial exploration, they often shut it down and never use it again. Instead of making them more productive, the expensive software just frustrates them and slows the process down. Why?

Because in purchasing the software, the clients put the proverbial cart before the horse. Project management software can look terribly confusing if you do not understand the language, methods, and standards of project management. But once you learn the underlying principles and skills, software like Microsoft Project will no longer be intimidating, and you realize how these types of tools can assist, not hinder, the planning process.

Here are the steps for creating a project schedule:

We need to:

1. Develop the Work Breakdown Structure (WBS).
2. Sequence activities.
3. Identify the project team.
4. Estimate duration of each task.
5. Identify the critical path.
6. Create a project budget.

Develop the WBS

The WBS is what the Project Management Institute calls the list of project deliverables and the components that go into each deliverable to complete the project. The deliverables are the "what" of the project, while the components make up the deliverables. (Project management pros refer to creating the WBS as "decomposing" the project—let them.)

A WBS is a deliverable-oriented grouping of project components that organizes and defines the total scope of the project.

—PMBOK 5.3.3.1

>> plan

When you start the WBS, you might not know all the deliverables and their components. Developing the WBS is a great time to brainstorm deliverables.

TOOL: MIND MAPS

We like to brainstorm using a mind map. Mind mapping allows you to come up with ideas without worrying about putting them in order. Here is an example of Olivia's mind map for deliverables. The project name goes in the center, the deliverables around the outside.

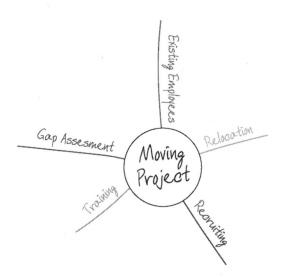

Once you have thought of all your deliverables, brainstorm the components of each deliverable. Let's take one of Olivia's deliverables: Relocation Package. What are the components? Among other things, Olivia will need to figure out housing options and a relocation package for each employee. So the new component mind map would look like this:

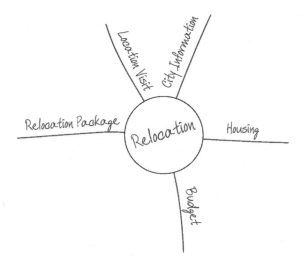

With your deliverables and their components on the map, you are ready to brainstorm the tasks or activities associated with each. Keep brainstorming all the actions you'll have to take to complete each deliverable. Here is an example:

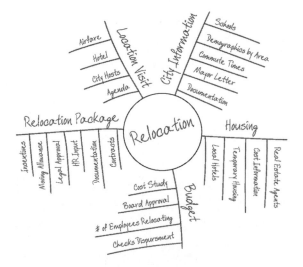

>> plan

Tool: Linear Lists

Some people find it easier to make a list of all the activities required to complete each component rather than a mind map. Use a pencil so you can erase and insert as things come to mind. Of course, making a list is easy enough if you are using your computer or tablet. Here is a short sample from one of Olivia's component lists:

Identify Activities on Relocation Package:

- Create a moving reimbursement budget
- Get key stakeholder sign-off on total budget and individual reimbursements
- Design document to communicate budget and moving plan
- Hold employee meetings to communicate budget and moving plan
- Design a moving contract
- Have all moving employees sign contract

Tool: Post-it Note Method

Some project managers like to use the "Post-it Note" method at this stage. This is how that works: List each component as a heading across the top of a whiteboard. Then have your team think up all the activities required to complete each component. Give each team member a Post-it Note pad to note each activity they can think of. Ask them to list only one activity per note and then stick them to the whiteboard under the proper heading. Of course you'll see a lot of duplicate ideas, which is great. Duplication indicates that an activity is a high priority. Once you are finished brainstorming, you can remove duplicates and reorganize them as needed.

No matter which approach you use, with this robust thinking complete, you are ready to flow all of the information into the Project Schedule.

Below is an example of a basic WBS (the real WBS for such a project would contain many more deliverables and components). The WBS creates an easy-to-follow map with all the necessary information to complete a project successfully. Now you can insert the components and activities into a Gantt chart, which becomes a project "scoreboard" of sorts that tracks progress on deadlines and ultimately enables you to deliver your deliverables. (A Gantt chart, named after its inventor, Henry Gantt, is a bar chart that shows when each task begins and ends and how tasks depend on each other. It's a valuable tool for creating your project schedule.)

	STATUS	% DONE	DELIVERABLES/COMPONENTS/ACTIVITIES	
2			RELOCATION	
2.1			Relocation Package	
2.1.1			Obtain HR Input	
2.1.2			Establish moving allowance	
2.1.3			Determine Incentives	
2.1.4			Draft Documentation	
2.1.5			Gain Legal approval	
2.1.6			Secure Contracts	
2.2			Budget	
2.2.1			Perform Cost Study	
2.2.2			Obtain Board approval	
2.2.3			Determine # of Employees Relocating	
2.2.4			Checks Disbursement	
2.3			Location Visit	
2.3.1			Establish Agenda	
2.3.2			Contact City Hosts	
2.3.3			Determine Airfare	
2.3.4			Secure Hotel	
2.4			City Information	

Example of a Gantt chart

Sequence Activities

Activities are the "how" that gets the "what" (the components) done. Now you need to sequence the activities to determine what needs to be done when.

When we ask people what we mean by "sequence," they always respond, "Put in chronological order." True enough, but that's only part of the sequencing process. You must also decide which activities must be done before, at the same time, or only after another task—these activities are called "dependencies."

DEPENDENCIES

A dependency is a task that is dependent on another task. If that sounds daunting, don't worry—chances are you have done this before!

Consider cooking a meal for a New Year's dinner. The star of the day will be a juicy, golden turkey. But before the turkey can make an appearance in the middle of your table, you will need to do a number of things.

First, you will need to buy the turkey. If it is frozen, you'll need to thaw it. Once you've thawed it, you will need to determine the method for cooking and then calculate the cooking time. Next you will need to cook it, let it rest, and carve it, and finally you will be ready to serve it.

It's not complicated, but how many cooks have panicked when they found the turkey was still frozen when it was time to put it in the oven? You can avoid problems like this when you understand "dependencies." Since you cannot cook a turkey until it is completely thawed, cooking is *dependent* on thawing. Now, let's clarify that dependency: A turkey has to be *completely* thawed. You can't make things go faster if you cook it when only partially thawed. If you try it, you'll just have to cook the bird longer. You'll still miss the deadline—and have a dried-out turkey to boot. So figure out which tasks are dependent on others—this is a crucial step toward hitting your deadlines.

We will come back to your turkey later, but you can now see that some activities are dependent on others, and that the proper sequence of activities is determined by dependencies.

>> plan

DEPENDENCY: *A logical relationship where two activities are reliant on each other's start or finish.*

There are a few types of dependencies. As an unofficial project manager, you will most often use the Finish-to-Start dependency. It is considered a "natural dependency" and is the easiest to understand and use.[1] Here is the definition of the Finish-to-Start dependency, along with definitions for two others you may encounter:

Finish-to-Start: Some activities are obviously sequential. If you build a house, the foundation goes in before the walls go up. These tasks are called Finish-to-Start because you have to finish the first task before you can start the next one. In addition, you might find use for the following dependencies.

FINISH-TO-START

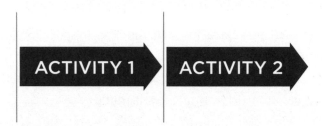

Start-to-Start: Some activities overlap. In this dependency, the start of one task triggers the start of another. For example, one person can be writing the second chapter of a book while someone else is editing the first.

START-TO-START

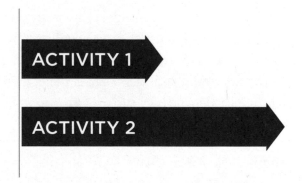

Finish-to-Finish: Some activities can't be finished until others are finished. A restaurant manager can't tally the total sales for the day until the last customer has paid the bill.

FINISH-TO-FINISH

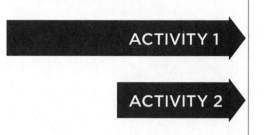

Try This at Home

Think about the principle of "dependencies" when you're doing day-to-day time and life management. If you applied this kind of thinking to your personal projects and even your weekly and daily planning regimen, how much more precise would you be in scheduling activities and achieving much better outcomes, whether planning a dinner, a wedding, or even a day's family outing?

Identify the Project Team

Now that you know what needs to be done, who's going to do it?

___

As she filled in her WBS, Olivia knew she needed to choose the right people for each deliverable, component, and activity, but it turned out to be a tough task. Knowing the importance of the project, Olivia had made a list of all of her team members' skillsets and realized she still had a few gaps.

"I'm going to add a few people to the team," she told the CEO as they passed in the hall.

"You just reminded me," he said as he stopped and turned around. "I need to talk to you about your team and so does HR. Can we meet this afternoon for five or ten minutes at three o'clock? Bring your list of existing team members and the new people you are hoping to add."

"Okay, that works." Olivia walked back to her desk. *This can't be good*, she thought.

She had the list in hand as she walked into a meeting with the CEO and the HR director.

"The first column represents the team members I already have," Olivia said as she handed them copies of the list. "The second column represents the additional people I am requesting. This group will be able to do everything we need to complete this project successfully."

"I see a couple of problems here. This is why I asked for the meeting," the CEO said. "As you know, there are a number of big projects associated with moving the company. Jeff and Bill are already working on my project, and now I need them full-time, and Maria has just been assigned to the finance project, so you are going to have less access to her."

Olivia was angry. Jeff and Bill were her best people. What would she do now, and why did the CEO just get to take them away? She didn't care if he was the CEO; he knew how important her project was. It felt like sabotage. She felt the anger rise.

Thankfully, the HR director broke in. "I hate to be the bearer of more bad news, but one of your new requests, Jevon, gave his notice last night. He won't be moving with us. In fact, he already has accepted a new position. He was very sad to go, but he just can't move his family right now."

With this news, Olivia remembered why she was doing this project in the first place. Everyone was overwhelmed. Everyone was making big decisions. Her anger subsided.

"Wow," Olivia said as she slumped in her chair. "I had no idea. I can't believe we are going to lose Jevon. He is such a great guy."

"Wow," the CEO echoed. "That is sad news." He turned to Olivia. "I know this is frustrating, Olivia, and I am sorry to take Jeff and Bill, but I have no choice. Without them, we won't have a new building to move into. Besides, I have faith in you. If anyone can figure it out, you can!" He stood up from his chair. "Thanks for getting me the list to review so quickly. Unfortunately, I have to go catch a plane."

"Okay, I get it," Olivia said, sounding a little defeated. "Thanks for taking a few minutes to let me know about the change. I will do what I can." She watched as the CEO left the room.

She was starting to feel overwhelmed again.

The HR director broke through her thoughts. "I've got some ideas, Olivia. If you have a few more minutes, perhaps I can give you more people to consider. For instance, I know you don't know Samir very well, but he would be someone I highly recommend."

"I'm willing to listen to any option," Olivia said with a halfhearted smile. "I really wanted to work with the people

I already know and trust, but at this point, I probably need to be more open."

Thirty minutes later, she walked out of the meeting with a list of team members—which the CEO later approved.

Though she didn't know everyone on her team, she now had enough people to assign to all the activities on the project schedule. She also knew that until the new people were up to speed, she would have to work even harder to ensure the project stayed on target.

Back at her desk, she laughed. Days before, she'd written the Four Foundational Behaviors on a Post-it Note and put it on her monitor. She hadn't even noticed it lately, but suddenly it was the only thing she could see. She thought back to all the emotions of the meeting: anger, frustration, being overwhelmed. None of these feelings had gotten the better of her. She read the note again: "Demonstrate Respect, Listen First, Clarify Expectations, Practice Accountability."

I think I'm finally getting this, she thought as she picked up the phone to call Samir.

———

The principle to remember here is "the goal defines the team," not the other way around. A common mistake is to assign whoever is available to the team instead of finding the right people for the job. A second mistake is lacking a clear project schedule, so that there is no "science" to assigning the right people to the right tasks.

A clear project schedule allows you to more accurately determine what human resources are required for what tasks.

In addition, with a clear road map you can build your informal authority with your team. You don't need to be the only one "assigning" tasks. You might have your team review the schedule with you and either volunteer for assignments or suggest other possible team members. In keeping with the Four Foundational Behaviors, when team members get to express opinions and offer ideas, it drives buy-in from your team, keeps them engaged, and motivates them to get the job done. They feel like they are finally on a winning team, instead of being assigned to some dreaded project team again. And, as in Olivia's case, it is not always going to go well. In many cases resources are tight and must be negotiated. An accurate project scope with the key stakeholders, a visual and detailed project plan, and your mastery of the Four Foundational Behaviors will put you in a position to influence others and to find possible hidden resources. This chart shows how to assign team members to components:

>> plan

	STATUS	% DONE	DELIVERABLES/COMPONENTS/ACTIVITIES	WORK HOURS	DURATION	START DATE	END DATE
1			RELOCATION	248	38 days	1 Oct	7 Nov
1.1			Relocation Package	116	33 days	1 Oct	2 Nov
1.1.1			Obtain HR Input	24	3 days	1 Oct	3 Oct
1.1.2			Establish moving allowance	6	2 days	4 Oct	5 Oct
1.1.3			Determine Incentives	6	2 days	4 Oct	5 Oct
1.1.4			Draft Documentation	16	4 days	6 Oct	9 Oct
1.1.5			Gain Legal approval	8	3 days	10 Oct	12 Oct
1.1.6			Secure Contracts	56	14 days	20 Oct	2 Nov
1.2			Budget	32	15 days	13 Oct	7 Nov
1.2.1			Perform Cost Study	16	5 days	13 Oct	17 Oct
1.2.2			Obtain Board approval	8	5 days	18 Oct	20 Oct
1.2.3			Determine # of Employees Relocating	2	1 day	6 Nov	6 Nov
1.2.4			Checks Disbursement	6	1 day	7 Nov	7 Nov
1.3			Location Visit	36	10 days	10 Oct	11 Oct
1.3.1			Establish Agenda	16	3 days	10 Oct	12 Oct
1.3.2			Contact City Hosts	8	5 days	13 Oct	17 Oct
1.3.3			Determine Airfare	4	1 day	17 Oct	17 Oct
1.3.4			Secure Hotel	8	5 days	17 Oct	17 Oct
1.4			City Information	34	6 days	13 Oct	18 Oct

Estimate the Duration of Each Task

Now that your WBS is in place, and you have sequenced activities and assigned team members to each task, the next step is to estimate how long each task will take. Then you'll know how much of the budget you need, what the actual schedule needs to look like, and whether or not you have the *right* team members on the right tasks.

The principle here is that "work" and "duration" are two different things:

Work ≠ Duration

Work is the time needed to accomplish a task. For instance, you might estimate that a certain task will take eight hours to finish, so you block out eight hours for it. But your "eight-hour block" may be totally unrealistic—how many people really have eight straight hours to devote to anything?

Duration is the time needed to get the work done, *accounting for everything else that needs to get done as well—real life.* We all have competing priorities: other projects to do and the rest of our jobs to take care of. So, upon further review, what *is* possible is scheduling one hour per day for eight days. The "duration" of the task is thus eight days, not eight hours. *Now* you will be able to accurately schedule the task into your plan and have a "built-in" mini risk management system.

Work drives our project budget, while duration drives our project schedule. For example, the actual work of writing the relocation plan for Olivia's project might take only a few hours, but the *duration* is just over a month. Why?

Because it will take that long to vet a relocation company, get approvals, write the plan, and get everything reviewed and edited.

Remember, time is one of the six constraints we mentioned in chapter three. Unreasonable deadlines can sink a project and often do. Be careful not to try to be a hero by scheduling tasks so tightly that there is virtually no "flex" or "float." Provide a little breathing space. By estimating duration accurately, you can come up with a realistic end date for your project.

However, upon review with the key stakeholders, you may well find they need an earlier end date. In fact, you may have experienced this before. If stakeholders tighten any of your constraints, you will want to negotiate. Using duration of activities instead of work for your time negotiation will provide you with some leverage for reaching a "win-win" with the stakeholders. Then go back to the team and tweak the duration of their activities in order to meet the agreed-upon date.

In Olivia's case, she has a hard-and-fast deadline for her project. She will do her scheduling by working backward from that date. This is a common project management practice. As she works backward, she will use the duration of activities to determine just the right recipe of time and resources to make her project a success.

In any case, don't promise to meet a goal you know you can't meet in the time allotted. Instead, have the "constraint priority" conversation if the duration of activities makes things a bit too tight. Your integrity is on the line, and it's more important than anything else.

›› plan

"There's nothing that
fills a development
team with horror
quite so much as
something along
the lines of 'the new
financial system will
be in place before the
end of the financial
year.' And when you
ask how that date was
arrived at you get little
more than 'that should
be enough time.'"
—THE ANGRY AUSSIE[3]

There is a "watch out" about duration. Experienced project managers remind us not to make task durations too long. Doing so creates a culture of procrastination, with folks waiting until the last minute to get their tasks done. In project management lingo, we call this phenomenon *Parkinson's Law*—people will work through the entire time allocated for an activity.[2] For example, if an activity most likely will take seven days to complete, and the project manager adds three more days to "play it safe"—scheduling the activity for ten days—then it will take the resources of ten days to complete that activity, with the team likely working overtime on that ninth day to get it done! It's just human nature.

So it is important to find the "sweet spot" when estimating the duration of a task. Learn how to be accurate with duration. There is no magic bullet for this, but here are a few suggestions:

1. **Draw on your own experience**. The more you work on building project plans, the better you get. During the closing phase of the project, a key project management skill is "templating" successes and talking through lessons learned. The next time you do the project, you will have an exact history to draw on.

2. **Ask a reference**. Don't be afraid to ask others what they have learned in a similar situation.

3. **Get advice from an outside expert**. Consultants provide great insights because they work with all types of companies, all over the world. It will often save you money in the long run to call on the knowledge of an outside consultant.

4. **Use the PERT formula to figure out how long each task will take**. You can estimate the time required for each activity using a project management tool called PERT (Program Evaluation and Review Technique). PERT helps you cope with uncertainty about activity completion times. To figure out how long a task will take, come up with three time estimates:

- Optimistic time: the shortest time in which the activity can be completed.

- Most likely time: the completion time having the highest probability.

- Pessimistic time: the longest time that an activity may take.

From these three estimates, you can use the following formula to calculate the expected time for each activity:

Expected Time = (Optimistic + 4 x Most Likely + Pessimistic) / 6

In PERT, the number 4 is a weighted average. It balances out the common tendency to make unrealistically short time

>> plan

estimates. The number 6 refers to the number of standard deviations between optimistic and pessimistic estimates.[4]

We can use Olivia's project to illustrate PERT at work.

The optimists on Olivia's team think the relocation plan can be completed in twenty-five days. The pessimists think it will take sixty. Olivia (based on overall team input) thinks it might take thirty-five.

So she uses the PERT equation to get a reasonable guestimate in keeping with the thinking of everyone on the team.

First she calculates 4 × 35 (most likely). Answer: 140.

Then she calculates (25 + 140 + 60) / 6. Answer: 37.5.

According to the model, Olivia needs to schedule 37.5 days to complete her relocation plan.

Estimate the duration of all the tasks on the work breakdown. Then you can schedule everything from the beginning to the end of the project. Here's part of Olivia's project schedule:

Annual Customer Event

	STATUS	% DONE	DELIVERABLES/COMPONENTS/ACTIVITIES	WORK HOURS	DURATION	START DATE	END DATE
1			RELOCATION	248	38 days	1 Oct	7 Nov
1.1			Relocation Package	116	33 days	1 Oct	2 Nov
1.1.1			Obtain HR Input	24	3 days	1 Oct	3 Oct
1.1.2			Establish moving allowance	6	2 days	4 Oct	5 Oct
1.1.3			Determine Incentives	6	2 days	4 Oct	5 Oct
1.1.4			Draft Documentation	16	4 days	6 Oct	9 Oct
1.1.5			Gain Legal approval	8	3 days	10 Oct	12 Oct
1.1.6			Secure Contracts	56	14 days	20 Oct	2 Nov
1.2			Budget	32	25 days	13 Oct	7 Nov
1.2.1			Perform Cost Study	16	5 days	13 Oct	17 Oct
1.2.2			Obtain Board approval	8	5 days	18 Oct	20 Oct
1.2.3			Determine # of Employees Relocating	2	1 day	6 Nov	6 Nov
1.2.4			Checks Disbursement	6	1 day	7 Nov	7 Nov
1.3			Location Visit	36	10 days	10 Oct	19 Oct
1.3.1			Establish Agenda	16	3 days	10 Oct	12 Oct
1.3.2			Contact City Hosts	8	5 days	13 Oct	17 Oct
1.3.3			Determine Airfare	4	1 day	17 Oct	17 Oct
1.3.4			Secure Hotel	8	3 days	17 Oct	19 Oct
1.4			City Information	34	6 days	13 Oct	18 Oct
1.4.1			Send Mayor Letter	6	2 days	13 Oct	14 Oct
1.4.2			Analyze Demographics by Area	10	3 days	14 Oct	16 Oct
1.4.3			Review Schools	10	3 days	14 Oct	16 Oct
1.4.4			Analyze Commute Times	4	1 day	17 Oct	17 Oct

For tasks that truly take only six hours in a particular day, you "round up" to one day as the minimum duration. This is standard procedure and provides you a little more slack for finishing the task. No matter how well you plan, there will be interruptions and crises that need to be handled. The better durations you come up with, the higher the probability of success.

> ### Try This at Home
> Think about the principle of "duration" when you're doing day-to-day time and life management. If you applied this kind of thinking and planning to everything in your life, how much stress would you avoid because you really know how long it takes to plan a surprise party, wedding, or dinner with the in-laws?

TOOL: MILESTONES

Another way to keep the project on track is to put milestones into your schedule. Like a traffic sign, a milestone is a signal that you've reached an important decision point in the project. Traveling down a road, you will see signs that tell you to stop, turn, exit, or go back. When you reach a milestone, you have to make that kind of decision—to keep the project going, stop it, back up, or change direction.

Milestones are up to you. For instance, if you feel the need to bring all the stakeholders back together on a given date, that's a milestone. Put it into your schedule. Milestone meetings are great for checking the health of your project at certain intervals.

Olivia did not want her key stakeholders worrying about her progress, so she scheduled specific milestones for her team and told the key stakeholders she would report on the progress of the project at the status report meeting.

"As you are all aware," Olivia said at the meeting, "we completed our first major milestone last week when we escorted to Dallas all of the employees still considering relocation. Though it was a logistical nightmare, we were able to accomplish exactly what we set out to do. Everyone got to explore the city, meet the relocation specialists, and get many questions answered. We even had dinner with the mayor, who gave a great listing of the reasons to relocate. I captured the list for those of you that missed it." Olivia passed the document around the conference table.

A couple of people commented on the trip, while others recapped the humorous speech the mayor delivered.

Olivia brought them back. "Our next milestone is to get the employees to make a decision about relocating. We need a count of who is staying and who is going."

"We need to know right away." This came from Vijay, a board member, who was always trying to push the deadlines forward.

"I know it is important," Olivia countered, "but the majority of the employees have asked us to extend the deadline. Since our goal is to have 80 percent relocate, I think we need to meet their request."

"We can't extend," Vijay fumed. "You listed this as a major milestone for a reason. We need to know who is moving and who is not. This information impacts how we proceed with the rest of the project." He was clearly frustrated.

"I realize that," Olivia said calmly, though part of her wanted to scream. *Did he think she didn't understand the potential impact?* Sometimes she wished he wasn't a key stakeholder.

She went on, "At the same time, if our goal is to have more people go with us, I think we need to extend the time. We have asked our employees to make some very hard decisions. Giving them another two weeks is a show of good faith."

"Two weeks!" Vijay was almost yelling now.

"That is what they've asked for." Olivia remained calm, though she was silently counting to ten.

"Two weeks *is* a long time, Olivia." This time it was the CEO who made the comment.

Olivia turned to address him directly. "Again, I knew this would be cause for concern. This is why we are having the discussion. I think the staff has made a reasonable request for more time. Giving them time increases our chances of people making the decision to move. But, I'm here because I want your input."

Olivia waited patiently as the room erupted in debate. Some people wanted no extension, while others, like the HR director, expressed concern that even two weeks would not be enough. After a few minutes, Olivia spoke again. "So, did we reach a consensus?"

Vijay looked up. He had been defeated. "It sounds like we need to give them more time. I just hope it does not backfire. Olivia, you should do what you think is best." Most of the room seemed to agree.

›› plan

"I appreciate this," Olivia said. "More time should make a big difference. However, I think we need to agree on the length of time before we leave the room. I don't feel comfortable choosing an extension without everyone's input. If we can agree, I can revise the milestone, and we will all have the same expectation. Anybody want to throw out a number?"

The CEO spoke before anyone else could. "Let's extend the deadline by ten days. This gives them a week and an extra weekend. We can see where we are at that point."

Olivia looked around for any dissenting comments or expressions, and when she saw none, she closed the discussion.

"Okay, ten days it is. I'll change the deadline on the milestone and report our continued progress next week."

Once you have created the project schedule, you're ready to move on to the next step: identifying the critical path.

Identify the Critical Path

Once you start executing your project, you'll be fighting the Bottleneck Monster. Remember that some tasks have to be finished before others can start (Finish-to-Start activities). Olivia can't start training new employees until they're hired. Eve can't stop infection from spreading through the hospital until she finds out why it's spreading. If one critical Finish-to-Start activity isn't done on time, you have a bottleneck.

That's why you need to know the "critical path" from one end of the project to the other.

The critical path is the longest way to get from the beginning to the end of the project, and the earliest and latest that you can start and end each task without making the project longer.

The activities on the critical path have absolutely no flexibility in when they begin and end. You can't start a task early because you're waiting for another task to end, and you can't finish the task later without making succeeding tasks late. If you miss any item on the critical path, you are at high risk for failure, resulting in cost overruns and missed deadlines.

>> plan

THE CRITICAL PATH: *The longest sequence of scheduled activities that must start and end as scheduled that determine the duration of the project. If any activity on the critical path is late, the entire project will be late.*

By understanding the critical path, you can see in advance where bottlenecks might occur and plan how to avoid or bypass them before they happen.

CRITICAL PATH

The series of activities that determines the duration of the project.

—*PMBOK* Glossary

Some people are a bit intimidated when they hear the term "critical path." It brings to mind all kinds of mathematical equations and complexity. In reality, the critical path is a tremendous high-value tool.

Let's go back to your holiday dinner. You already determined the activities you need to do to get your turkey ready. Which of these are on the critical path? Which will negatively impact your celebration if you don't get them done at exactly the right time? One key milestone sits squarely in your critical path: Dinner starts promptly at 4 P.M.!

With this deadline in mind, we can start to identify the critical path activities for preparing our bird.

TASK	DURATION	COMMENTS
Buying	Anytime from about 3 months ahead.	You can buy the turkey at any time and still make your deadline. To get the best price, you might buy it 3 months in advance.
Thawing	36 hours	You need to know the exact number of pounds in order to determine how long to thaw the turkey (three hours per pound), and once thawed your turkey needs to go directly to the cooking stage. Let's assume you're preparing a twelve-pound turkey. You can estimate that it will take thirty-six hours to thaw. This will be a critical path item
Determine the method of cooking	Up to you	You can determine this long before.
Calculate the cooking time	Up to calculation	You can do this as soon as you know how much the turkey weighs.
Preheat oven	1 hour	You can start preheating while the turkey thaws.
Cooking	2.6 hours	Without the proper cooking time, you will find yourself with a bunch of sick guests. We will estimate thirteen minutes cooking time per pound for our twelve-pound bird: 13 × 12 pounds = 2.6 hours. This will be a critical path item

TASK	DURATION	COMMENTS
Resting	0.5 hours	You can estimate a thirty-minute rest period after the turkey has finished cooking This will be a critical path item
Carving	0.2 hours	You can put the turkey on the table right at 4 pm and carve each piece as you serve it to your guests This is a critical path item
Arrange tables and chairs	0.5 hours	We can perform the next three table-setting activities while the turkey is cooking
Position tablecloth and centerpiece	0.25 hours	
Set china and silverware	0.25 hours	

>> plan

By adding the estimated durations of the Finish-to-Start relationships for all of our project activities, we can determine that we *must* start the first critical path activity—thawing the turkey—39.3 hours before our project completion deadline of 4 P.M. We'll need to start the thawing activity no later than 12:42 A.M., two mornings before our big event. If we start any of the critical path activities late, our dinner also will be late!

Are all activities on the critical path? No. Those not on the critical path represent what we call "slack" or "float."

You can see the turkey dinner critical path visualized in the following Gantt chart.

It is easy to calculate the critical path of more complicated projects with project management software. To find the path requires accurate dependencies, durations, and start/finish dates.

PROJECT SCHEDULE

TURKEY DINNER

	DELIVERABLES/COMPONENTS/ACTIVITIES	PRE-DECESSOR	WORK HOURS	DURATION	START DATE	END DATE	WHO
1	TURKEY PREPARATION		40.3 hours	40.3 hours			Mom
1.1	Thaw turkey		36 hours	36 hours	Dec. 31	Jan. 1	Mom
1.2	Pre-heat oven		1 hour	1 hour	11:42 AM	12:42 PM	Mom
1.3	Cook Bird	1.1, 1.2	2.6 hours	2.6 hours	12:42 PM	3:18 PM	Mom
1.4	Rest Turkey	1.3	.5 hour	.5 hour	3:18 PM	3:48 PM	Mom
1.5	Present Turkey, Carve and Serve	1.4, 2.3	.2 hour	.2 hour	3:48 PM	4:00 PM	Mom
2	TABLE SETTING						Teen
2.1	Arrange Table and Chairs		.5 hour	.5 hour	2:30 PM	3:00 PM	Teen
2.2	Position Tablecloth and Centerpiece	2.1	.25 hour	.25 hour	3:00 PM	3:15 PM	Teen
2.3	Set China and Silverware	2.2	.25 hour	.25 hour	3:30 PM	3:45 PM	Teen

Gantt chart time axis:

- 1/1/15 4:00 PM
- 1/1/15 3:30 PM
- 1/1/15 3:00 PM
- 1/1/15 2:30 PM
- 1/1/15 2:00 PM
- 1/1/15 1:30 PM
- 1/1/15 1:00 PM
- 1/1/15 12:30 PM
- 1/1/15 12:00 PM
- 12/31/14
- 12/31/14 12:42 AM

Once you understand the critical path, you will assign the best and most engaged human resources to the critical path activities. This is no place to assign new or disengaged employees; if you do, you will significantly raise your risk. You need your best resources on the critical path so that you have the highest probability of completing these tasks correctly and on time.

And remember, most project team members are not working on just one project. They have other priorities, bosses, fires to put out, and the rest of a job to do. Many times life just gets in the way, and it becomes challenging for them to complete tasks on time. By keeping your eye on both critical path and slack items, you will be able to shift resources from the slack activities to critical path items in trouble.

Finding the Critical Path Using the Gantt Chart

You can also pick the critical path right out of a Gantt chart by highlighting all the tasks that must start and finish as planned. They will generally be the dependencies you set up in your WBS. Remember, you already did deep thinking and planning around the dependencies. The better job you do on the dependencies, the easier it will be to chart the critical path. This is another *great* reason to use project-planning software like Microsoft Project. It will highlight the potential critical path for you based on the input you provide about dependencies and activity start-and-finish dates.

Use these tips to avoid bottlenecks on the critical path:

- *Best people.* Put your most trusted, talented, reliable, and engaged people on the critical path instead of the slack. Which core team members do you trust to get things done on time?

- *Cross-training.* Make sure more than one person can do critical path tasks—this means you ought to train people to do more than one job if the project schedule and budget permit. Who will do Task A if the best person to do it gets sick or drops out?

- *Micro Team Accountability Sessions.* Do mini check-ins as often as needed to ensure deliverables are on target. Micro meetings will help you spot bottlenecks and minimize the fires that ruin project plans. (You can find a deeper discussion of Team Accountability Sessions in chapter five.)

With a little practice, the project schedule can help you to beautifully manage your projects. An accurate schedule will help you create a budget as well, which is the next step in the project planning phase.

Create a Project Budget

In many cases, unofficial project managers may not have to create a budget, particularly on smaller projects. Even if you are not responsible for the budget, it is important and helpful to be able to think about the costs of your project. Your key stakeholders will be much happier if you take your financial responsibility for the project seriously.

The Four Foundational Behaviors are at play here, too. When you are fiscally responsible, you will be seen as *demonstrating respect* for the organization's mission and critical outcomes and *listening* to its needs. You will be *clarifying expectations* in connection with the company's financials and holding everyone and yourself *accountable* for staying within the guidelines of the budget—even when you are not specifically asked to create one.

Create your project budget under two headings: external expenses and internal expenses. Your external expenses include everything you will need to buy from sources outside your organization, like materials, equipment, and consulting services. External expenses include any bill from an outside supplier.

Your internal expenses include all the time you've allotted for each core team member and other people you need from inside your organization. To calculate your internal expenses, multiply the work hours for each person by his or her job category's hourly cost:

$$
\begin{array}{lcr}
\text{Ali's hours} & = & 40 \\
\times \text{ Ali's hourly cost} & = & \underline{\text{US\$500}} \\
& & \text{US\$20,000}
\end{array}
$$

Add up the costs for everyone, and you have your internal expenses.

Sum your external and internal expenses, and the total is your project budget. But don't stop there. Add 10 percent for miscellaneous expenses. Of course, make sure you disclose this contingency funding to your key stakeholders.

> Project Manager: "Here's the budget we need."
> Boss: "What can you do for half the money?"
> Project Manager: "Fail."

Usually, you don't have to make up a budget from thin air. If you or your organization has done similar projects before, you probably already have data on the cost of goods and services for those projects, as well as a project plan. We will talk about this more in the Close process group (chapter seven), where you archive data and best practices.

For example, Olivia knows roughly what training one new employee costs in materials and labor hours. She can easily forecast what it will cost to train the new employees, once she knows how many new employees there will be.

On the other hand, back at the hospital, Eve has never done a project like this before, so she doesn't have that kind of data. But she can find out what her team members cost per hour, along with pricing the materials and services she needs from outside vendors. Most of her external expenses will probably come from hiring consultants and researchers. Chances are if Eve is responsible for a project budget, she can get access to the data required for accuracy. For official project managers, budgeting is a science; but for an unofficial project manager like you, these few tips should be enough to help you create a usable budget.

An accurate Gantt chart, fiscal vigilance, and mastery of the Four Foundational Behaviors—these are the elements of a successful project plan.

DEVELOP A COMMUNICATION PLAN

A project manager's job is 90 percent communicating with team members, stakeholders, executives, suppliers, and the media—in meetings, conference calls, emails, text messages, reports, and websites. That's a lot of communicating, and you can go crazy from communication overload if you don't have a plan for managing it. This communication plan is the last priority of the project's **Plan**.[5]

Your project will not succeed without the right communication to the right people throughout the life of the project. In this day and age, we never want to assume how people want to communicate. Many projects are being done virtually and globally, and there are many modes of communication, so we must adopt a solid communication system.

COMMUNICATIONS PLAN

Communications planning involves determining the information and communications needs of the stakeholders: who needs what, when they will need it, how it will be given to them, and by whom.

—*PMBOK* 10.1

>> plan

We started to build this system in the key stakeholder interview back in **Initiate**. Now that we are in **Plan**, we have solidified the key stakeholders, the project team, and the project plan and budget, and we need to make sure we have an overall communications road map.

———

Eve was shy. She didn't like to bother people with her problems, and she liked to do things on her own. Her independence was a good thing—up to a point. Although she made a rock-solid project plan, she simply overlooked committing people to a communication plan.

Before long, her project was way behind schedule. People just weren't cooperating. She couldn't get the core people on the nursing teams to report their findings, the financial people didn't keep her posted, and the doctors were too busy to talk. Worst of all, she couldn't get her supervisor's attention so she could get some help. In addition, she heard some buzz around work that people felt like they were not getting information from her. That surprised her. She thought she was doing a pretty good job. Because there was no specific communication plan, no one communicated in any direction. It was very painful for Eve to think no one really cared, and even more frustrating because she could not move the project forward, even though she had developed a great project plan.

Eve needed an effective communication plan to keep the project visible.

———

Most key stakeholders want to know a project's status and how they can help. Executives often want a variety of communications about the progress of your project. And team members need to know about their own progress.

When developing your plan, think about how people want to receive communication. What if you need to get hold of someone? What is the best way? It may no longer be email or phone. Perhaps some of your key stakeholders or team members prefer texting. Others might like your organization's instant messaging system. Knowing the preferred method of communication for each of the people you have to communicate with is yet another way to mitigate project risk. In short, make a communication plan that works for you and the members of your team.

TOOL: PROJECT COMMUNICATION PLAN

Eve clearly needed a communication plan. First she decided to set up several different ways to communicate—email, live meetings, and video conferences—depending on the audience for the message. Not all of her team was on-site, and in a busy hospital meetings are hard to hold, so email and video conferencing made sense. Next she determined what types of communication were needed—for example, updates on how the research was going and the overall status of the project—along with how often they needed to occur and which delivery method was best. Then she settled on who would be responsible for overseeing each type of communication. Eve's detailed Project Communication Plan looked like the one shown on the next page.

COMMUNICATION PLAN

Project Name: Customer Acquisition Plan

Date: 10/11

Prepared by: Eve

WHAT	WHO		HOW	WHEN
COMMUNICATION TYPE	INITIATOR	AUDIENCE	METHOD/CHANNEL	TIME/FREQUENCY
Research Updates	Research Team	Core Team - Key Stakeholders	Reports via Email	Updated Every Tuesday
Team Accountability Session	Eve	Project Leader	Virtual Meeting	Weekly on Tuesday Noon
Status Report	Eve	Core Team - Key Stakeholders	Video Conference	At each milestone

After you create the communication plan, share it with your team and the key stakeholders. Insert reminders about communication events in people's calendars. Remind yourself to update the reminders. And above all, make sure you follow through on the plan—if you don't keep your own commitments, you will give people permission not to keep theirs.

TO SUM UP ◑

PLAN Skillset and Toolset
> TOOL: Risk Matrix

> **Skill:** Plan a Risk Management Strategy
> TOOL: TAME the Risks
> TOOL: Risk Management Plan

> **Skill:** Create a Project Schedule
> TOOL: Mind Map
> TOOL: Linear Lists
> TOOL: Post-it Note Method
> TOOL: Gantt Chart

> **Skill:** Develop a Communication Plan
> TOOL: Project Communication Plan

The better you plan, the more likely your project will succeed. That's just a basic reality. You might be skeptical about plans, but you know deep down that it's better to plan than to start a project without counting the cost.

Don't expect things to go according to plan. Sometimes people will not get things exactly right. Executives and others won't do what they said they would do. Team members may miss commitments. Stakeholders will want to change things just when you thought you were gaining speed on the project. Use your risk management, communications, and project road maps to stay true to your journey. As the detours come up, you will be in a great place to better handle them than if you just wandered around back roads hoping to find your way.

CHECK YOUR LEARNING— PLANNING THE PROJECT

✓ How do you manage risks?

✓ How do you break a project down into manageable pieces?

✓ How do you schedule project deliverables and their associated components?

✓ How do you identify necessary resources?

✓ How do you identify communication channels?

CHAPTER 5

EXECUTING THE PROJECT: CLEAR THE PATH OR FALL ON YOUR FACE?

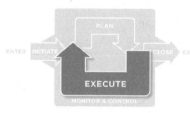

EXECUTE Mindset:
Engage people through consistent and shared accountability.

C ARL LOVED HIS JOB COUNSELING international students at a Swedish university. He helped them get started in their new school and oriented to the town. They came from all over—China, South America, eastern Europe, Pakistan, and Ukraine. They were all smart but solitary, and he worried about their isolation. The local students had their own friends, but the foreign students didn't associate with one another. They all kept to themselves.

One in particular, Marta from Albania, never spoke to anyone. She was thin and so cold all the time she almost upholstered herself in leather to stay warm. Silent and unapproachable that was Marta. Just smile at her, and she'd walk away.

To Carl, students like Marta were missing out on the main reason for going to school abroad—to live in a different culture and get to know diverse people. So he went to his director with an idea: "I'd like to figure out a way to get Swedish and international students together so they can make some connections." He suspected the director didn't approve of him (it was probably his beard), and he was a little hesitant to talk to her. She was one of those people who are "highly organized," so she asked Carl to bring her a project plan.

I don't know why everything has to be a project around here, Carl sighed to himself. *My students aren't "projects."* But as he lay awake that night thinking about it, he started to see a kind of vision of what could be done. And it *would* be a project—a big one.

Instead of getting the international students involved with the locals, he would get the locals involved with the internationals. He would call it the "Capitals" project. His idea was to divide the entire student body into national groups. Each group would have a club room called the "Capital" where the groups could mingle and get to know the culture of that nation with food and drink, music and dances, presentations, and arts and crafts—with the international students at the center of each group.

Some capitals were easier to visualize than others. *How about a whole club room called "Paris"? Think of the pastries, the café music, the artists.* He had at least twenty French students on campus. The Italians would have a "Rome" room, the Brazilians a "Brasilia" room. Then there was Marta, his Albanian. *What is the capital of Albania?* he wondered. *Who knows, but they must have one, and they've got to eat and drink. And Marta will have to get involved—she can't refuse.*

It was a brilliant idea, his director said the next day. She told him to move ahead with the project plan.

Carl did a great job interviewing stakeholders, creating a scope statement, recruiting a project team, and building a project schedule (his highly organized director required all of that). The first milestone on the schedule would be a big kickoff party for his core team members: Arne and Hank from the graphics department could do publicity, and two professors from the languages faculty could be heads of this and that—but mostly the team was made up of the international students themselves. *It's going to be great!* he thought.

Carl hosted the big party. Everybody had drinks and clapped for him. The director complimented him on his plan, and he went home happy.

But he wasn't happy for long.

THE PRINCIPLE OF ACCOUNTABILITY

Like Carl, after **Initiate** and **Plan**, you now know the scope and direction of your project. You know exactly where you're going, with a clear road map and schedule to get there. You might even be excited; after all, the rest is just execution. Simple.

But what does it take to execute successfully as a team?

In a word: accountability. Successful project leaders practice accountability because it reinforces informal authority and ensures project success. Successful leaders hold people accountable because it is the right thing to do, even when it's hard. If you don't practice accountability, people won't think you're serious.

How often do we get asked to do something at work that nobody actually cares about? When we take on assignments, accept meetings, and make commitments, we silently ask ourselves, "I wonder how much this really matters?" and then we wait for proof that it does. Great project managers prove that every request, every commitment, every missed deadline matters. And in doing so, they earn high levels of respect and follow-through from the team.

> "Nothing destroys trust faster than making and breaking a promise. Conversely, nothing builds trust more than keeping a promise."
> —STEPHEN R. COVEY

Most people don't understand the principle of accountability. They think of it as negative. When they hear the word "accountability," they see Mom or Dad sending them to bed or the boss standing ominously in the office door. They think "performance appraisal" or "annual review."

In your role, you're not practicing that kind of accountability. As an unofficial project manager, you likely don't have much formal authority over your team members anyway. The principle of accountability is simple: When you keep your commitments, you become a trustworthy human being. You gain the trust of your team members, who will be encouraged to keep their commitments as well. You also gain the trust of your stakeholders, who will be motivated to keep their commitments to you. You are living the definition of informal authority when you inspire people to *choose* to play on your team.

And the more commitments you keep, the more people are likely to give you the benefit of the doubt when problems arise—as they inevitably will.

By your own behavior, you tell people how much you value accountability. As we said in chapter two, the days of "do what I say, not what I do" are long over. You must model the behavior you want from others, consistently. You must keep 100 percent of your commitments to the team, key stakeholders, and the project.

By keeping your own commitments *with precision,* you can consistently hold other people accountable. Just one person on the team not pulling their weight can throw the project way off, so you need everyone engaged and contributing their best. It might surprise you, but strict accountability makes them *more* engaged, not less.

Projects often stumble because people stumble. They get lost, they run into roadblocks, they get diverted. Your job as leader is not to manage them but to help them manage themselves. That means "clearing the path" for them, making it possible for them to keep their commitments. You engage people through consistent and shared accountability.

How many great projects are launched with applause and banners and T-shirts and giveaway pens, and then they just fade away into the memory like an old holiday at the

>>> execute

beach? Maybe you even find the pen in your drawer one day and you think, *Whatever happened to that project?*

Most likely it happened the way it happened to Carl.

———

A few days after the party, Carl was busy entertaining a group of Mongolian professors. Then he had to catch up on a pile of student applications. Ten days went by, and he thought it might be a good thing to follow up on the Capitals project plan. He rang Arne and Hank about getting started on the publicity, but they were both out. So he sent some emails.

Then one of his students got sick. Then it was a public holiday. Then there was the final exam crunch and the Christmas break. A few of his team members contacted him about the project, but he was too busy to call them back. *I'll just pick it back up after the New Year*, he thought.

But after the New Year, Carl was swamped again with "Arrival Days" for new international students. One day, the director passed him in the corridor and asked in her best directorial voice, "How is the Capitals project coming along?" Mentally, he slapped his forehead. Physically, he smiled confidently, assured her all was well, and walked away very fast.

Carl had simply failed to hold himself accountable for his own project. He thought about all the energy he put into his key stakeholder interviews and the great project schedule he had put together. It all looked good on paper, but he blamed himself for not adhering to the very timelines he had created! You could argue that nobody else followed through, either, but it was Carl's job to manage the project, not theirs. Now, Carl had good reasons for his failure to execute. As he told himself, everything he had done instead of the project had needed to be done—no question about that. After all, an excuse makes total sense to the person who makes it.

But the project was now nearly three months behind schedule, and nothing had been done. Carl had two choices. He could drop the project and hope no one would notice. Or he could pick up the pieces and lead it to success.

When that afternoon he saw Marta sitting by herself, sipping coffee in a corner of the commons and trying not to see the other students walking past her, he knew what to do. He would pick up the pieces.

>>> execute

Like Carl, you won't execute without a shared system of accountability. There's no getting around that. Even well-intentioned people who do want to help need someone to hold them accountable. So . . .

- How do you create team accountability?
- What do you do if a team member doesn't keep a commitment?

To answer these questions, you need a mindset of consistent, frequent, regular, shared accountability. You also need to know how to use informal authority to help team members keep their commitments.

Create Team Accountability

Have you ever had a teacher, coach, or mentor who cared if you succeeded? How did he or she keep you engaged? Millions of us take piano lessons and play sports but never grow up to play the piano or become skilled athletes. Why not? Maybe the internal motivation isn't there, but there's more to it—most of us lacked a teacher or coach who knew how to engage us.

**THE WEEKLY CADENCE—
ARE WE WINNING OR LOSING?**

We recommend regular weekly meetings, with the key numbers posted on a whiteboard or computer desktops so that everybody can see them. With the numbers up there, potential trouble spots surface quickly.
—Joe Knight, Roger Thomas, and Brad Angus[1]

The leader who engages us has clear, high expectations and *cares* if we meet them. She respects us and shows that she values us as people. She understands our situation and helps us solve our problems. And she *regularly* and *often* holds us accountable for what we say we'll do.

Carl had to commit himself to the project first before he could help others get committed. Determined to see it through *this* semester, he revised the project schedule and called a core team meeting for Monday.

Only a few people could make it. Carl expected that. Some of the people he called had only the vaguest memory of what he was talking about and begged off. He could understand that; he would just have to find somebody else to fill each of those spots.

But he talked straight to the people who did come. "I blew it," he acknowledged. "We did a lot of good planning, but I didn't follow through, and I'm sorry. I still think this project is really important, so I'm committing myself to it.

"I want to get together every Monday at this time for a team accountability session. It'll be short. We'll review where we stand with the project plan overall. I'll report where I am with completing my commitments, and you will report on yours. We will work together to make sure we stay on track. If you run into problems, I will commit to clearing the path for any issues that may be outside your control.

"Can you commit to that? Once a week?"

"Sure," they said. Carl knew it wouldn't be that easy, but it was a start. They went over the revised project schedule and made specific commitments to move the project forward.

"We're on our way," Carl said, relieved.

> ### PROJECT MANAGEMENT PROVERB
> "A cadence of visibility and accountability produces not only reliable results again and again, but also a high-performance team."

By scheduling a weekly accountability session, Carl set up a *cadence* of accountability. A cadence is a steady rhythm. Have you ever worked on a team that felt "in rhythm" or "in the flow"? How would you describe it?

>>> execute

This cadence is the key to excellent execution. A team in cadence is going to win. Everybody knows what's expected when, and how to achieve it; no one person is responsible, no one person gets the glory or takes the fall. Everybody is moving forward together; anyone who needs help gets the whole team's support.

TOOL: TEAM ACCOUNTABILITY SESSION

You can create this rhythm of accountability by holding a Team Accountability Session each week throughout the life of the project.

This meeting is totally different from the typical "project status meetings" you know about. This chart illustrates the differences:

TYPICAL "PROJECT STATUS" MEETING	TEAM ACCOUNTABILITY SESSION
• We listen to other people (or pretend to) drone on about what they've been doing. We doodle or play on our phones.	• We focus on the project schedule and budget. Are we where we're supposed to be? If not, why not?
• If it's a teleconference, we get our other work done (or mute the phone and take a nap).	• We focus on how we can help each other and clear the path when necessary.
• We make excuses or blame other people for our lack of progress.	• We commit to doing specifically what's necessary to get the project back on track / keep it on track.
• We waste hours on this meeting.	• We do it quickly and stick to the agenda.

The Team Accountability Session is not long, maybe twenty or thirty minutes max. It's a quick, high-focus huddle to see if we're winning or losing—mostly to find out if we're on track or if anybody needs help. One highly effective project manager holds these sessions to "let everyone working on the project see exactly how they're doing and harness their ideas about how to fix whatever goes wrong. Something always does."[2] Some people refer to this powerful meeting as the "un-meeting."

Depending on your project, you may need to hold the Micro Team Accountability Sessions or check-ins we referred to in chapter four for specific phases of your project. You and your team will determine how often they are needed. Micro sessions *are not* just another reason to meet. They *are* intended to keep control of specific deliverables on the critical path.

One organization we worked with held a micro session twice a day, every day, at 9 A.M. and 3 P.M. They were monitoring progress on the production of machine parts. Each part took less than a day to make, but each was crucial to the project. So twice a day, a small subset of the core team met to ensure the required part had been produced. In addition, they made sure the machinery team had everything they needed to complete the next part on time.

Micro sessions may be required for specific phases of your project. They usually won't require all team members to be present, and they don't replace your regular Team Accountability Session held weekly with your core team.

This weekly cadence keeps core team members from feeling isolated and reminds them that the activities they have been assigned are needed contributions, not "just a job" to fill time. The success is in the sum of the parts,

>>> execute

providing that everyone can constantly see the goal line. And because lots of problems arise when you're carrying out a project, nobody should feel like they have to solve them alone. Seth Godin has this insight: "As the project gets built, our instinct is to hide. Hide our roadblocks, our mistakes, our worries. As we hide, we keep the rest of the team in the dark. As the darkness settles in, it's easier than ever to keep hiding, because to unhide now is double the trouble."[3]

The Team Accountability Session is designed to do a few very specific things:

- Enable the team to see the project as a whole by reviewing the entire project plan.

- Require team members to report on the commitments they made the prior week.

- Keep the project moving as team members make new commitments each week.

- Give insight to the project manager on where she needs to clear the path.

TEAM ACCOUNTABILITY SESSIONS

Status review meetings are regularly scheduled meetings held to exchange information about the projects ... held at various frequencies and on different levels (e.g., the project management team may meet weekly by itself and monthly with the customer).

—*PMBOK* 4.2.4

Keep a record of each Team Accountability Session. See how Eve used the following tool to record the meeting:

TEAM ACCOUNTABILITY SESSION

Project Name:

Project Manager: Date:

REPORT ON LAST WEEK'S COMMITMENTS

MAKE NEW COMMITMENTS

CLEAR THE PATH

OTHER

With this tool, she could follow up on all the team commitments each week. In this case, Eve's team could see immediately that they were on schedule except for one deliverable: Patient Reminders.

Early in the project, they had discovered that hospital staff often forgot to wash their hands as they moved from one patient to another, resulting in the spread of infections. So one project deliverable consisted of signs everywhere asking, "Did You Wash Your Hands?" The reminders appeared on the walls in the hallways, the restrooms, the doctor's offices, the hospital entrances and exits—wherever there was a blank space.

It wasn't enough. The posters worked fine on visitors, but the staff got so used to them that they weren't even seeing them anymore. The project team had anticipated this, so they had also planned to ask the patients to remind staff members to wash their hands.

"The patients aren't doing it. It's that simple," said Micaela, one of the patient resource people. Micaela's job was screening patients at the front door of the hospital, and her assignment on the project team was to carry out all the tasks that had to do with the patients themselves. One of her tasks was to make sure every patient knew to remind staffers to wash their hands. "Some of our older patients don't understand what we're asking them to do. And other patients are too timid to ask a doctor or a busy nurse, 'Have you washed your hands?'" Micaela said.

Dr. Saltas didn't like this. He stared at Micaela. "Look, we all agreed the patients were the last line of defense. It's in their own interest to ask. This topic is pointless. Let's move on."

Eve didn't have to point to the Four Foundational Behaviors she had posted on the wall right over her head (partly because of Dr. Saltas). Everybody knew they were there, and Eve knew her job was to be the example.

"We're a team. Micaela has a task to do and she's having trouble with it. Ignoring this won't get us the right end result. What can we do to clear the path for her?"

The room got quiet. Then Mario, the public relations director, spoke up. "We could have badges made up for everybody—'Ask me if I washed my hands.'"

The head of nursing chuckled and said, "I'd love to see the nurses wearing those, and I think they would if I asked them to."

Dr. Saltas was still miffed. "Badges," he snorted. "Just another germ carrier."

"That's true," said the consultant.

The head of nursing replied, "It doesn't have to be. We already wear ID badges—we can just add the reminder to the badge. And I think the nurses won't have any problem reminding patients to ask the doctors to wash their hands." She smiled at Dr. Saltas.

"Let's do it," came the low voice of Dr. Leron, the head of the medical staff.

Eve agreed. "Micaela, I will work with you offline to determine the next steps."

Think about how that meeting went. It wasn't all smooth. Maybe meetings never can be, but that's okay because you want different opinions and emotional engagement. Everyone in the room made good points. Some people got irked. Eve did her best to keep the discussion respectful—and it all turned out pretty well. She was careful not to dictate a solution to the problem. She facilitated the discussion and let the team work out both the solution and their individual commitments to it. Her team is in the game and, even with some bumps along the way, they are clearly playing the game together to win.

Let's be real—it's not always going to go perfectly, is it? There will always be issues, right? What are some issues that might come up in a Team Accountability Session that could hinder your project schedule?

Could Eve have done better? More empathy, maybe? No doubt, but the meeting fulfilled its chief purpose: to find out where the problems are and get everybody's best thinking on how to solve them.

But, you say, you can't always do that in twenty or thirty minutes. That's true, but it's usually enough time to review the plan, account for the previous week's successes, and commit to the few activities that are crucial to staying on track. Do some problems need more attention? Sure. In those cases, call a separate project meeting to focus on them, or get together with those who are affected or most likely to solve them. But the brief Team Accountability Session is essential—never skip it.

Says one experienced project manager, "Set up a short mandatory weekly meeting where each team member takes a minute or two (no more!) to tell the team what they did last week, their plans for this next week and any roadblocks the team can help with ... This creates urgency for each individual on the team around making progress every week."[4]

> "If I stagger and lose the way, you must help me, you must keep me on the true path."
> —LEO TOLSTOY

Holding Others Accountable

Now, what if you have a problem with a team member? Somebody who's always negative (like Dr. Saltas) or who doesn't pull their weight? Has that ever happened to you?

What happens to the project when team members fall apart on you?

You have lots of choices. You can remove them from the team, shame them, reprimand them in front of the rest of the team, or ignore them and hope they go away—but none of these reactive choices meet the requirements of "informal authority." Instead, you can hold them accountable through all Four Foundational Behaviors. When you forget to practice respect, you *might* win the battle but you *will* lose the war.

When things get hard to handle with a team member, all types of emotions arise, particularly disappointment, anger, and frustration. If you let these emotions crash down on the individual team member or even the whole team, you have *really* lost the war.

Have you ever hit the "send" button on an email when you're angry? It feels great in the moment, but later you find yourself wishing you could "recall" it. How much damage has that done in your professional and personal life? It's okay to feel disappointment, anger, and frustration, but a great leader can *manage* that set of emotions to get the greatest results.

Ever hear the phrase "Count to ten before responding"? Practice this before you hit "send" on a team member. You might be surprised how well it turns out. Remember, your job is not just to finish a project—it's also to build a great project team. And that means building people up, especially when times get tough.

So how *do* you hold people accountable who aren't holding themselves accountable? You must first hold *yourself* accountable to the Four Foundational Behaviors. You start by *demonstrating respect*. If you react negatively, you'll violate the rules of informal authority. You will lose the inspiration required for the team to win. No one likes to feel ashamed; fearing your reaction, your team will disengage

Suppose a team member comes to the meeting and says he or she just couldn't keep a promise this week. First, what is the downside of doing nothing about it? What are you teaching the team? You're teaching them that commitments don't matter. Once you

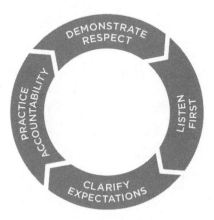

let your commitment standard slide, you no longer have a standard. If one team member consistently misses and you do nothing, others will start to miss, too. And what about the people who keep their commitments? They start to lose respect for *you*.

So the first time someone misses a commitment, use the Four Foundational Behaviors to find out what's getting in the way:

1. **Listen first.** Let the team member describe why the commitment was missed.

2. **Demonstrate respect**. Be empathic about the situation.

3. **Clarify expectations**. Restate the commitment; update the deadline for completion.

4. **Practice accountability**. Let the team member know the team counts on everyone's commitments. Each commitment made is integral to project success.

By consistently holding people accountable *in* the meeting, you accomplish two powerful things:

- The team member will "own" the problem; he will understand that he let the *team* down, not just himself or you.

- The rest of the team will watch this and think, *I never want to put myself in that position.*

This is pure accountability on the team level. All team members strengthen their resolve to bring their best selves to this team and the project.

This solution may not work every time. What if you have a chronic problem with a team member who doesn't keep commitments? You will have to take the next step: an "accountability conversation" either in front of the group or in a separate one-on-one meeting. Team members need to know you are handling the situation, so say something during the accountability conversation—and do it in a way that demonstrates respect while communicating that a lack of follow-through is unacceptable and jeopardizes the project's success.

>>> execute

Team Accountability Sessions

The team does only three things in a Team Accountability Session:

1. Focus on the team scoreboard: Are we meeting the goal? Are we on schedule?
2. Report on commitments from last week in a "lightning round."
3. Make new commitments: "What can we do this week to move the score forward?"

Going back to Eve's project, after two weeks Micaela kept coming to the accountability sessions with one excuse after another. She couldn't get the new badges done because she had to spend the week with a visiting team of hospital inspectors. The next week her apartment was being painted, and she had to be there.

Eve said, "I know there are lots of demands on you, Micaela, but that's true of all of us. Here's the impact on the project schedule: We're going to be at least a month late with our numbers. We won't know if what we're doing makes a difference or not, and that means more patients will have problems.

"We make these commitments to each other, and we need to know that we can count on you. Is there more we can do to clear the path for you?"

What do you think? Did Eve show *respect*? Did she *listen* with empathy? Did she *clarify expectations*? And is she holding Micaela *accountable*? How would you have handled it differently?

First, she acknowledged that, like everyone else, Micaela has a busy life. There are always competing urgencies and emergencies, but when we make a commitment to the team, it's personal. Micaela needs to keep up with the rest of the team. She reminded Micaela of how important the project is and the impact of her own contribution. Then she asked if the team could count on her to meet her commitments.

Some team members will need a straightforward and gentle reminder now and then *in front of the team*. If someone flakes out and you just let it slide, what are you communicating to the rest of the team? How seriously will they take their own commitments? How loyal will they be to the team? How will they feel toward people who slack off?

Your own resentment will build up, too, if you don't talk about it straight and with respect. "When we fail to set boundaries and hold people accountable, we feel used and mistreated," says Dr. Brené Brown, one of the great students of how people behave in the workplace. "This is why we sometimes attack who they are, which is far more hurtful than addressing a behavior or a choice. We need to understand that it's dangerous to our relationships and our well-being to get mired in shame and blame, or to be full of self-righteous anger."[5]

On the other hand, if you do what Eve did, you're communicating that everyone is accountable and that everyone's contribution matters. You're also holding on to your own integrity, and that matters more than anything.

>>> execute

Team development on a project is often complicated when individual team members are accountable to both a functional manager and the project manager. Effective management of this dual reporting relationship is often a critical success factor, and is generally the responsibility of the project manager.

—*PMBOK* 9.3

Hold Performance Conversations

Occasionally, you will need to hold a one-on-one Account-ability Session in private. This is called a Performance Conversation. Here is an example:

Carl had asked Marta to be on the core team for the Capitals project. She always came to the accountability sessions, but (as Carl expected) it was very hard for her to carry out her tasks because she was so afraid of people. Three weeks in a row she failed to follow through.

"Marta, this is the third week you have not completed your commitments," he said. He was calm and respectful. "Can we talk after the meeting? I'd like to understand what is happening." The rest of the team who had been watching closely let out a sigh of relief when Marta said, "Yes, I would like that, too."

"Great," he said with a smile as he turned to the next team member. "Kris, how did you do last week?"

Anticipating that Marta might miss again, Carl had already prepared a Conversation Planner (depicted later in this section). As he sat in his office, he looked over it one more time. Marta knocked on the door. "Hi," she said meekly.

He stood up from his chair, offered a warm smile, and invited her to sit. "Marta, thanks for coming. I think you know I want you to have the best possible experience you can get here. The reason I want to talk to you is to make sure that happens. When you miss commitments to the team and then fail to follow through, we can't achieve our goals for you or the project. A lot of students like you are alone, a long way from home for the first time. That's why we are doing this project. Not only is the team counting on you, the other students are, too. We need your help. When you say you'll do something, you need to follow up. You've missed three weeks of commitments, and now we are all behind schedule." Marta shrugged a little. Carl sat back and waited. And waited. Finally, Marta spoke up in a voice he could barely hear.

"I have trouble," she said. And that was it—for a while. After another few more minutes, "I have trouble talking to strangers. I don't know what to say. The language barrier is hard."

Carl waited.

Marta went on. "I feel foolish. I want to help," she said in broken English. "I want to have friends here. But it's harder than I thought. I don't want to let the team down, and you are right. When I don't do what I said I would, it doesn't make them want to know me more. I know this."

Carl had wondered for weeks how to get through to Marta and had wanted to understand why she was so passive. In just a few minutes of empathic conversation, he found out the root of the problem and how to clear the path for Marta. But he wanted her ideas first.

"What can I do to help?" he asked.

"Maybe . . . someone can go with me."

Carl already had the right person in mind—another team member, Professor Oleson, a young French-language teacher who liked hanging around with the foreign students.

"Marta, I can find you a helper, but I need you to catch up on your commitments to the project. Can you?"

"Yes." Marta nodded, almost eagerly. "If someone can help me with the language, I will catch up on everything."

———

>>> execute

What do you think about the way Carl handled this Performance Conversation? He explained why he wanted to talk. He talked about his concerns respectfully and got right to the point. He reminded Marta what was at stake. He listened with empathy to her concerns and feelings. Instead of solving the problem for her, he asked her opinion about what to do. And then he did what a good project leader does—he figured out a way to clear the path for her.

Meanwhile, back at the hospital:

Eve was worried about Dr. Saltas' effect on the team. His negative attitude was consistent and pervasive no matter how many times she respectfully tried to deflect it in front of the team. She knew she would need to have tougher one-on-one Performance Conversations with him. The first thing she needed to do was get her emotions under control. She found him so frustrating, and she was worried her disdain for his attitude would just show up in her approach. So she sat down at her computer and planned her conversation to make sure she had a win/win approach and an anticipated outcome. She used a Conversation Planner to help frame her thinking.

TOOL: CONVERSATION PLANNER

The Conversation Planner tool will help you plan a Performance Conversation. A guide for how to approach each item in the tool follows.

CONVERSATION PLANNER

With whom?   When?

WHAT IS MY INTENT?

Explain why you want to have the conversation. Your intent should be to build up the person as well as to move the project forward.

WHAT ARE THE FACTS?	WHAT IS THE IMPACT?
THEIR POINT OF VIEW, MY POINT OF VIEW	ON PROJECT, PEOPLE, PROCESSES
Explain the facts: commitments not kept, meetings missed, negative behaviors or attitudes. Then listen empathically to the situation from the other person's point of view.	What is the person's behavior costing the project in terms of relationships and outcomes?

ACTION ITEMS	BY WHEN
Write the person's commitments.	

>>> execute

WHAT IS MY INTENT?

The Conversation Planner asks you to define your intent first. Why are you asking for the conversation? There are two reasons this is a critical step. First, you don't want the other person to wonder about your agenda. Second, you want the person to quickly and clearly understand that the conversation is only about the outcomes of the project—not character or personality. You do not want to give the team member a reason to think, *Oh, Eve just doesn't like me very much, that is why she is picking on me.* So make sure your intent is clear.

WHAT ARE THE FACTS?

Next, think through the facts you need to share. Make sure you are prepared to provide an example or evidence of the behavior at issue or mistakes made.

WHAT IS THE IMPACT?

Be prepared to articulate the impact these facts have on the project so the team member clearly understands the big picture.

Have the Conversation

Getting really clear on how your end of the conversation will go is a great way to "calm down" and communicate in exactly the right way. Be logical, clear, and above all, *demonstrate high respect.*

Clearly, and in a firm but inviting tone of voice, state your intent and the facts. This is *clarifying* the problem. Then pause. This is a crucial step. You need to give the team member time to process the information and let it sink in. Then listen to his or her point of view on the facts.

Be empathic. Put yourself in their shoes and understand their point of view the best you can. Then sit back and be quiet. If you listen quietly, you'll give the other person a chance to get their emotions out in the open and "decompress"—you don't have to agree, disagree, or defend yourself—and you might learn something, too. Just listening gives you a chance to find out *why* the person isn't performing.

ACTION ITEMS

Once the person feels like you understand them, ask them for suggestions on how to solve the problem and start *clarifying expectations*. Usually, they'll know what to suggest; in any case, lay out in clear and specific terms what you expect from them and what they can expect from you. *Practice accountability* by agreeing on specific action items, and set an appointment for reviewing progress on those expectations. Make sure the other person knows you'll be following up at that meeting.

These conversations are not necessarily easy, but if you rely on the Four Foundational Behaviors, your informal authority will grow as the team members find they can talk meaningfully with you.

––––––––

Now let's see how Eve handles a Performance Conversation with the stubborn doctor on her team. This is going to be tough. Note how she declares her intent, states the facts and the impact, listens, and clarifies expectations.

"Dr. Saltas, I want you to know how much I respect your experience and knowledge. You can add so much to the project. My intent in this conversation is to find out how we can both help this project succeed.

"Frankly, I'm worried about the negative feelings you create on our team. I think people are intimidated by you, and I feel like it's affecting the project. When you were talking to Micaela in our last meeting, it sounded to me like a personal attack. When you criticized nearly every idea in our brainstorming session two weeks ago, I saw people shut down and refuse to participate. I think this is a pattern of behavior.

"Also, when we ask you to take on a task, it seems to me you change it so it isn't helpful. For example, when you came back from the infectious disease conference, you were going to bring the materials so we could read them. Instead, you just told us it wasn't worth your time and there was nothing worth sharing.

"Here's how it affects the project. People won't speak up or share ideas when you're there, and we don't feel like we can count on you to follow through."

Eve paused to let Dr. Saltas digest the information and saw the blood drain from his face.

"Dr. Saltas, I stated a few things, and now I would love to hear from you. What do you think about what I have said?"

Eve sat back and braced herself. She had never believed she could talk to a doctor like that, especially one with so many initials after his name there wasn't space on his office door for all of them. But she felt good about it—she'd laid out the facts, she'd been respectful, and she was putting the project first.

The doctor went on a rampage. Everybody around him was incompetent. That conference was worthless. The project was hopeless. "You're never going to stop people who are already immune-compromised from getting sick. The ideas you've come up with will just make things worse. Nobody has a clue how to stop HAIs. You're just wasting time and keeping me from doing my job."

Eve didn't say anything to this. She tried to put herself in his place—and didn't really get there—but she'd worked with doctors for a long time and knew it was important to them to feel respected. They spent years and years on their education and sacrificed a lot to get where they were, and it was all life and death decisions from then on. She understood it was a stressed-out man talking.

He took a breath, then said, "I can't keep working for three bosses. I just can't."

Having no idea what this meant, she just nodded with empathy and invited him to continue.

"Dr. Leron, who doesn't like me. You. And then the consulting work the hospital wants me to do. I'm too strung out. It's too much."

"Oh, you have consulting work, also?" This was the first she'd heard of it.

"Yes, the board wants me to represent the hospital. We're a team of consulting surgeons. We go around the country advising emergency clinics. I'm gone every weekend, and it seems like I never see my family."

"You never go home?" Eve was starting to understand his crankiness—he was terribly overcommitted. "And the project?" she asked gently. "Do you have any suggestions? Do you want to drop out?"

"No," he sighed. "It's important, I know. We need to do something. Actually, I have a few ideas about the surgery ..."

It was strange, but maybe all Dr. Saltas needed was to get all those pressures off his chest. In a quieter voice, he started talking about some things the surgical teams might do to cut back on HAIs. He offered to run some experiments himself. Eve wrote it all down, and they planned a time when they could go over the results together.

As he was leaving, Dr. Saltas said he was sorry about the tantrum and bad performance, and shook Eve's hand. "I know you're just trying to do your job," he said.

"We're doing it together," she replied.

"Would you mind if I spoke to Dr. Leron about your situation?" Eve asked.

He was quiet for a moment, and said, "Whatever you want." Then he was out the door.

As we've noted, one big issue most unofficial project managers face is that their team members don't report to them. This was part of the problem here—Dr. Saltas was serving too many masters.

A few days later, Eve met with the medical head and described the stresses Dr. Saltas was experiencing. She told him the HAI project was at risk because of it. Dr. Leron had a lot of respect for the man (but not much warmth) and promised to ease up on him.

———

We've seen how this method works for hard conversations, but the Conversation Planner can be used to plan positive conversations, too. You might be asking, "Why would I ever need to plan a positive conversation?" Sounds a little silly, right? But think back to the last time someone gave you positive feedback. It's very likely you heard something like "Good work!" or "Nice job!" Though you walked away feeling great from the compliment, you may have also wondered to yourself, "Which part of my work was good?"

You will take the power of informal authority to a whole new level when you have the skills to deliver positive feedback in the right way. You do this by declaring your intent and sharing the facts and impact of the good work. When you tell people exactly what they did that was great and the impact it had on results, you give them everything they need to replicate the good work. Reinforcing specific positive actions by your team members is a sure way to get momentum on your projects.

>>> execute

Samir sat outside the conference room. He was waiting for Olivia, who had called and asked to meet him there. He wasn't sure what the meeting was about, but he was not worried. Olivia was a great project leader. He knew she would clarify everything when she arrived.

"Samir!" Olivia had turned the corner and was walking toward him with a stack of papers. "Thanks for waiting. It has been a crazy day."

Samir grabbed the door and some of the papers as they walked into the room. "No problem. What's up? Do you need me to do something more on the project?"

"No," Olivia said. "No new assignments today. In fact, I called you here to tell you thank you."

They both sat down, and Olivia pulled a folder out of the stack. "Samir, you did really great work on the relocation package, and we've been so busy I didn't want to miss letting you know what a big impact you've had on this project."

Samir was smiling, but he felt a little uncomfortable, too. No one had ever called him to a formal meeting just to thank him for something.

Olivia went on. "There are a couple of specific things I noticed while you were working on the relocation plan. First, I was so impressed with how you engaged Lisette and Tim. In fact, they mentioned to me how much they enjoyed working with you. They told me you were clear about what was needed, that you checked in with them regularly, and you stopped to help them when they were off track. As a result, the three of you fulfilled all the deliverables, and you met the deadline. Impressive stuff!"

Samir's discomfort had disappeared. Pride was all that he was feeling now.

"One more thing," Olivia said. "After working so hard, I'm sure you were exhausted. You had every reason to take a break from the project for a day or two, and I wouldn't have thought anything of it if you did. Instead, you came to me and asked what we needed now. With Jerome on sick leave, we were falling behind in the training plan, but because you were willing to pitch in, we were able to get back on track."

"It was nothing," Samir said. "I wanted to help the team."

"You did," Olivia said. "You've been making high-impact contributions every step of the way. I just wanted you to know your work has not gone unnoticed. Thank you, Samir. I'm so glad you are on my team."

Olivia shook his hand and stood up. "I'm off to the next meeting."

"Thanks," said Samir. "I know you are busy. I really, really appreciate your taking some time for me. And thanks for the 'Thank you'! It was not at all what I expected and such a nice surprise."

>>> execute

———

The next time you acknowledge someone for a job well done, try using this formula:

- Intent
- Facts
- Impact

A powerful thank-you means so much more than a ten-dollar gift card, *and* the recipient will know exactly how to replicate the good job they've done. The chances are very high they will.

TO SUM UP ⊙

EXECUTE Skillset and Toolset

➤ **Skill:** Create a Cadence of Accountability
   TOOL: Team Accountability Session

➤ **Skill:** Hold Performance Conversations
   TOOL: Conversation Planner

By now, you can see that executing the project is all about engaging people. You can have the most sophisticated project planning and processing, but people are still in the middle of it—people with jobs, families, and personalities. Plus, they all have bosses of their own—and if you're an unofficial project manager, most likely you're not one of them. But that doesn't matter. Executing is only accomplished by mastering the skills that help people invite their best selves to the party. They will choose to bring their best for a leader who inspires and encourages them.

But if you do a good job of keeping your team in cadence the way we've described in this chapter, you have a better chance of delivering on time and on budget. Above all, keep the Four Foundational Behaviors in mind—they are vital at *Execution*, as you've seen.

As a very wise project manager puts it, executing your project "depends on what people—those imperfect, opinionated, stubborn biological entities—decide to say and do, day in and day out."[6] You might not be the boss, but by following the principles in this book, you can have a lot of influence over the decisions the people on your team will make.

CHECK YOUR LEARNING—
EXECUTING THE PROJECT

✓ How do you keep people engaged throughout the project?

✓ How do you create team accountability?

✓ How do you give effective performance feedback?

>>> execute

CHAPTER 6

Monitoring and Controlling the Project: Keep Your Sanity or Lose Your Mind?

MONITOR AND CONTROL Mindset: *Drive progress through transparent communication.*

O LIVIA COULD NOT AFFORD TO miss a step. Even though everything looked good, the project felt shaky to her. Many of the employees were still deciding if they would relocate, and until they did, she couldn't finish hiring replacements. So Olivia spent most of her time monitoring and controlling the parts of the project she could control.

KEEPING TABS ON THE PROJECT

The group of processes called Monitor and Control is about making sure the project goes as planned—on time, on budget, and with quality. To monitor and control is to watch out for anything that can set the project back. As one project manager said to us, "Good control reveals problems early—which means you'll have longer to worry about them."

MONITORING AND CONTROL

Monitoring and control is the process of keeping track of the identified risks ... to determine if risk responses are as effective as expected, or if new responses should be developed. Risk control may involve choosing alternative strategies, taking corrective action, or re-planning the project.

—*PMBOK* 11.6

The Monitor and Control processes are about being proactive. If you are doing a great job monitoring and controlling the procedures and systems you already set up, you are also equipped to handle changes to the project that will arise. Change requests might be inevitable, but you can keep things reasonable. Projects often fail because of scope creep, which, as we mentioned, can drive you crazy.

And it's not just the fault of those asking for more "stuff." Scope creep happens because the scope may have not been clear in the beginning, or because the project leader may be saying "yes" to changes without thinking through the implications. Sometimes the project leader cannot think the implications through because the basics to measure against are not in place, and the project becomes a free-for-all.

Project leaders often stumble because of two opposite management approaches: abandonment and micromanagement. Some ineffective project managers abandon the team, leaving them to struggle on their own. We have seen managers who mean well abandon the team intentionally, believing that it is "tough love." They think the way to develop people is to leave them alone. Nothing could be less helpful. Keeping a vigilant eye on the team and the scoreboard is essential. Once you have set clear expectations, you need to monitor and measure the team's progress to see if the game is being won or lost. On the other hand, micromanaging project leaders get too deep into the details and crush team members' initiative. Still others do both—they abandon the team for a while and then dive back in to play the hero when things go wrong. Effective project managers steadily monitor progress and control the project to stop it from drifting into chaos.

Monitor and Control surrounds all the other process groups. Why? Because if we have followed all the guidelines in the other groups, we are already monitoring and controlling with vigilance. Think about it: In **Initiate**, we monitor our key stakeholder group, keeping communications open. We've clearly defined the Project Scope Statement, and we're measuring the team's progress against it. In Plan, we monitor and control risk. We have our project schedule, and we are using it to monitor the progress that aligns with the project

>>> monitor & control

scope. In Execute, we use the Team Accountability Session to monitor the team's performance and engagement levels to control timelines and quality of work.

If we Initiate, Plan, and Execute well, it will be easier to Monitor and Control the project.

Keep Stakeholders Informed about Project Status

One expert says, "The main reason for conducting project status reviews is to identify significant variances from the project management plan and to ensure that corrective actions are taken to get back on track."[1] In other words, if you want to keep key stakeholders happy, you need to check in with them regularly and often. They need to know if you're making progress, or, if not, what you're doing about it and how they can help.

———

In the sixth week of Olivia's project, things were going smoothly. The relocation plan had been carried out on time, and other deliverables for the project were on target, too. Then a huge problem arose. Based on the milestone meeting with key stakeholders (described in chapter four), Olivia extended the employee notice for relocation deadline by ten days. Though many of the employees had not turned in an official decision, it looked like about 50 percent of the staff was going to make the move. Olivia was working her plan based on this premise. On the day of the deadline, a number of people came to her office and tearfully resigned. Moving their families would be harder than expected. By the time the day was over, she realized only 20 percent of the staff would relocate.

This was a disaster. Olivia was sad to lose so many great colleagues and friends, and was totally unprepared to hire and train 80 percent of the staff. So Olivia took the problem to the team.

"We are never going to make the deadline," her best team member said.

"And what about all the support for our clients?" another team member asked. "With so many good people gone, our clients are going to feel it."

"What about our training budget?" asked another. "Did we plan for this?"

"No," Olivia answered. "We based the number on 70 percent of the staff relocating. I could never have predicted this was going to happen."

Olivia didn't know what to do. Up to now this project had been her shining moment, and she feared she had blown it. She realized the emotions of the day were getting the best of her.

"Let's take a break," she said. "I need to go back and look at the project schedule. And I probably need to meet with a few of the key stakeholders to let them know what has happened."

Samir, who was now one of her favorite team members, spoke up. "I've been managing the relocation budget. With so many people staying, we will be able to reallocate that money."

>>> monitor & control

"You're right, Samir," Olivia said as she realized she hadn't even thought of this yet. "And we did build this possibility into our risk management plan, so I need to go back and look at the strategy." Things were looking up already.

Olivia addressed the team one more time: "I need you to think about how we can still meet the desired results for this project. I know it seems overwhelming right now, but we made a good plan. There has to be a way. I will alert the key stakeholders and see if they have any suggestions as well."

Olivia went back to her desk and sent a request for an immediate status review meeting with her key stakeholders.

———

The project manager drives progress through transparent communication. What do we mean by "transparent"? "As project managers, we were hired to tell the truth and include the good, the bad, and the ugly in our status reports," says one expert. "Sugar-coating project issues and problems for management will only get us in trouble later. Don't make excuses … Don't be afraid to deliver bad news. Just make sure when you present management with issues and problems with your project you have a plan to get it back on track."[2]

World-class project management expert Matthew McWha of the Corporate Executive Board says, "There's a lot of perceived personal risk in saying, 'I'm managing a failing project' … Or people actually think they can turn it around, so they don't bring it up. They think they're better off trying like the dickens to recover it in the meantime."[3]

In keeping with the principle of transparent communication, Olivia explained the predicament straight out to the key stakeholders. Though she and the team had perfectly executed the relocation plan, it hardly mattered now—and the hiring and training of so many new employees had barely been on her radar. She didn't want to report that her project was in serious trouble, but the principles of respect and accountability required it.

TOOL: THE PROJECT STATUS REPORT

The project status report is a "talk document." It's not just a formality, but a chance to get the help you need to stay on track—so the status report is a real benefit to you as project manager. An expert said, "All customers want their jobs finished on time and on budget—or preferably faster and cheaper. But if they can't have that, and sometimes they can't, what they really want is to be kept informed along the way."[4]

THE PROJECT STATUS REPORT

The status report describes where the project now stands related to schedule and budget metrics; what the project team has accomplished; and future project status and progress.

—*PMBOK* 10.3

Who should receive a status report on your project? How often and in what form? Start with your communication plan. Identify which stakeholders require a status report and how you can best give it to them.

Let's take a look at a Project Status Report template you might find useful:

PROJECT STATUS REPORT

Project Name:　　　　　　　　　Date:

Prepared by:　　　　　　　　　　Prepared for:

OVERALL PROJECT HEALTH

☐ ON TARGET　☐ AT RISK　☐ IN DANGER

DELIVERABLES	ON TARGET	AT RISK	IN DANGER	NOTES

CLEAR THE PATH	ACTION	WHO	DATE

This report can keep all key stakeholders abreast of what is happening. It's also a way for you to get any obstacles to your progress cleared away. This does not have to be a complicated document or loaded with red tape. It can be an "at a glance" document so key stakeholders and others can easily and quickly understand if they are winning or losing.

The Overall Project Health checkboxes act like traffic lights, so you need to determine if each deliverable is green, yellow, or red. If the project or a deliverable is on target, the light is green—full speed ahead. If it is at risk, that's a yellow light, and you need to slow down and pay attention. If it is in danger, you've hit a red light. Stop and carefully consider what to do next. Don't be like the project manager who said, "We haven't got time to stop for directions—we're already late."

A red or yellow light is a signal to stakeholders that you need their help. It means you've got a problem with resources, timelines, or budget, and you want to provide the key stakeholders with some options for them to clear the path for the team. Sometimes a stakeholder can get something done with the stroke of a pen that the project manager can't do alone. Proactively providing suggestions to solve problems will speed up this process.

Make sure you state the problem clearly in the report. "Written reports should be written like the headlines of a newspaper," one expert advises. "A summary of a project team's accomplishments, pending and potential problems, and plans ... are all that are needed."[5] You should also bring ideas for solving your problems.

———

>>> monitor & control

At the meeting, Olivia explained that the project was in danger. She described her situation in the project status report and reassured everyone that she was looking for a solution. The stakeholders were disappointed, and most of them were sympathetic, but they were still adamant that nothing about the actual project results could change.

"I know the results are important, and my team and I are still committed to meet your original expectations. The good news is, I considered both of these risks. I even have a plan in place. But, even as I planned for the risk, I never imagined we would have so many new hires and so much training to do. Though we have a few ideas to minimize the problem, we may still need more resources."

"That's not acceptable!" This came from Vijay, who was pushing his chair away from the table. "The new building has already set us back. We've got two major projects running here. They can't both be going wrong!"

"I understand your frustration, Vijay, but this team has nothing to do with the building project," Olivia countered.

"Yes," the CEO said. "Let's try to reserve our frustrations about that one for the right project manager." This made some people smile since the CEO was managing the building project.

The finance person spoke up. He looked directly at Olivia. "At least some of the resources you need can come from the relocation budget. If I am doing my quick calculation right, you'll be using less than half of the relocation money. And it sounds like you have some other ideas in mind."

"We thought of that," Olivia said, "but I still don't know if it will be enough. Not only will I need to contract for more training, we are going to need another recruiting company. In fact, we've already begun that search. My team is working on a few additional creative solutions, but I wanted you to know the score right now. At least for the moment, we are off track. And, I may need some additional help."

The CEO said, "I propose we give Olivia a chance to find further solutions. I know she will do her very best to maximize her resources. In the meantime, I'd like to ask the finance team to help her crunch the numbers. With so many people leaving, there might be more in the budget than we realize."

The meeting ended, and Olivia felt hopeful. She was happy for the help from the finance team and even more appreciative of the support from her CEO. However, the deliverables had not changed. She would have to count on her team to come up with some creative solutions. Most important, she had laid all her cards on the table. Some of the stress was gone because the key stakeholders were aware of what she was trying to manage.

———

Project status reports are not just for crises. The reports are essential to the cadence of accountability, providing regular updates to key stakeholders. Just letting them know how things are tracking can keep key stakeholders calm and connected to the project—and your level of informal authority will continue to rise. You will be seen as a true leader of the project, accountable and transparent in both the good and the not-so-good times.

MANAGE SCOPE CHANGE EFFECTIVELY

One of our consultants started to fix a leaky shower in his bathroom, but being an idiot at plumbing (his words), he more or less broke the thing. Fixing the broken shower required new tile work. "While we're at it," said the tile guy, "why not retile the whole bathroom?"

"Okay," our friend said. "Why not?"

But while retiling the bathroom, they broke through into the kitchen wall.

> "Anything that can be changed will be changed until there is no time left to change anything."

Let's make this story short. Six months and US$140,000 later, our friend had a new bathroom *and* a new kitchen, which he likes very much. But it wasn't in the family financial plan, and the payments will go on and on and on.

What began as a simple project to replace a leaking pipe turned into a monster that ate our friend's bank account. Every project is liable to get out of control like this and consume you. What you thought would take six months turns into three years. What you thought would cost x turns into x times x times x!

Controlling Scope Creep

As we mentioned in chapter three, we could be driven round and round in circles by what we call scope creep as the original project grows gradually out of control. Preventing it is called "scope change control," or "keeping the monster in its cage."

Your reputation as a project manager depends on doing things on time, on budget, and with quality, so you'll want to avoid letting people, especially your own team members, add a new feature to the project every time they have a new idea.

CONTROLLING SCOPE CREEP

Scope change control is concerned with (a) influencing the factors that create scope changes to ensure that changes are agreed upon, (b) determining that a scope change has occurred, and (c) managing the actual changes when and if they occur.

—PMBOK 5.5

Of course, you cannot and should not avoid all changes. Market conditions, customer needs, executives and their priorities, technology—everything can change overnight, and you can't be the cop who arrests everyone who is trying to change anything. So where do you draw the line?

Today, particularly in the IT world, projects require us to iterate and adjust to conditions that can change on a dime. As an effective project manager, you need a method to deal with change. You must be agile. In fact, "Agile" is a term for a project management process that was born out of a need to be more than "just in time."

>>>> monitor & control

Your projects probably don't require you to implement the technically sophisticated Agile system, but you do need to be ready for change and nimble about it. We live in a synergistic world, where people do change their minds and even come up with *better* ideas that lead to better outcomes. At the same time, we live in a world where people get rewarded for coming up with good ideas, and sometimes you need be skillful in pushing back respectfully.

How do you tackle change requests respectfully? Besides the obvious—stay calm, keep your head—you need to stay neutral until you have gathered the facts. Think back to the Conversation Planner, because the same rules apply here:

- What is the intent of the change?
- What is the impact?
- What would be required to make the change happen?

You can't make a rational argument for or against any change until you know the answer to these questions. If you sound like you're whining when you push back, then you know your argument isn't rational.

The one thing that will usually convince a powerful scope creeper is money.

A consultant in our company shared this amazing tale:

Terry was working as a project management consultant to a large fast-food chain. The project team had created marketing and advertising billboards showing appetizing pictures of their menu items, and they were in a final review meeting. Much of the collateral and signage had been printed.

As they showed the images to the entire team, one senior vice president raised a point. "These images are great," he said. "However, the burgers only have one pickle. I really think they need three."

After the executive left, the team despaired. The change would mean a lot of work, missed deadlines, and a blown budget. One guy threw a chair across the room. Why? Because the unspoken rule in this organization was to implement any recommendation made by a senior vice president—that meant despite all the costs, all the time, all the effort, the team would have to redo the marketing collateral and add "three pickles on every burger."

But Terry encouraged the team to follow a project change-management process.

With a change-management tool to guide them, they took time to determine the impact this change would have on their project. They considered the impacts to deadlines, budgets, and scope. They discussed whether or not three pickles actually made the marketing better. They figured out what resources would be needed to make the change and discussed any risks making the change would pose both internally and externally.

With the facts in hand, they scheduled a meeting with the vice president to show him the report. The Project Manager opened, "Thanks for taking some time to meet with us today. We are preparing to proceed with your request to add more pickles to the images for our marketing project. Before we do, we thought you might appreciate knowing the impact of the change."

>>>> monitor & control

She handed the vice president the project change report, which documented all the facts they'd collected. It said that the cost of adding two pickles neared US$50,000.

The vice president sat in stunned silence, shaking his head. At last he said, "I had no idea. I really thought this was an easy change, and I'm embarrassed to think how much money I have cost this organization over the years every time my colleagues and I have had an opinion."

Since the project manager had the right information, she was able to have a professional and coherent conversation with the vice president instead of whining about his interfering. Because of transparent communication, the project manager was no doormat—she got the right result, *and* in a very short time changed the project management culture of that organization.

———

In this case, the vice president decided not to make the change. However, he could have looked at all of the facts and just as easily have said, "Do it!" The project change request process is not intended to avoid change but to evaluate proposed changes so that you make only those that give you better results.

How can you tell if a change makes sense or not? How do you know if the pickles are that important? You need a change process, so when people come to you and say, "Hey, wouldn't it be good if we could just add this?" you'll have a system to help you decide if it *will* be good.

TOOL: PROJECT CHANGE REQUEST

Use the following proactive-thinking tool to evaluate how a proposed change affects the project. It is based on the "constraint model" as a filter for understanding the impact of a change.

PROJECT CHANGE REQUEST

Project Name:

Request made by: Date:

PROPOSED PROJECT CHANGE

REASONS FOR THE PROPOSED PROJECT CHANGE

HOW THIS CHANGE WILL AFFECT THE PROJECT CONSTRAINTS

Time

Scope

Quality

Resources

Budget

Risk

KEY STAKEHOLDER APPROVAL

NAME:	**DATE:**
SIGNATURE:	
NAME:	**DATE:**
SIGNATURE:	
NAME:	**DATE:**
SIGNATURE:	

monitor & control

Make sure you first clarify expectations with the proposer of the change. Cycle back to your stakeholder interview questions to ensure you have the specifics of the change. Then document the change request, along with the reason for it, and take that information back to your team. Think with the team through each of these constraints: How much time will it take? How much more money? How many more people and resources? What are the risks of changing things now? What about timelines? Work out how best to get the change accomplished. Be courageous enough to have this conversation with the proposer, and, if necessary, the key stakeholders. You will be surprised how apt they will be to listen when they realize you are looking out for their and the organization's best interests.

Once your project change request has been planned out and is complete, share it with your stakeholders so they know what's going on. If they agree with the changes, they will approve them by signing the project change request form. If they don't agree, you can document the reason for the denial and keep it in your records, should the subject come up again.

"The worst thing you can do," experts say, "is save up all the change orders as the project goes along and present them to the customer at the end. If you do that, you are likely to face a serious backlash."[6]

The change request form requires deep thinking, but don't worry. You don't need to fill it out for every change, but it does give you a thinking process to follow when somebody suggests one. A small change here and there is one thing—you can shrug it off or take it on—but the principle of accountability means that you think through big changes using this process.

And be careful even about small changes, because you can get nibbled to death if they start to mount. "You need to settle on a specification and be ruthless about delivering things from the core list before allowing others to be added in," says one expert. "Usually developers are good people who will bend over backwards [to accommodate new requests]. If you multiply this out, it can lead to significant non-delivery down the track."[7]

SCOPE CREEP VERSUS SCOPE DISCOVERY

Eve knew that the harmful *C. diff* bacterium lives everywhere—on sinks, floors, and doorknobs—and that it's usually harmless except to people who are old, sick, or on heavy antibiotics. But in her hospital the disease was attacking people of all ages. They had just quarantined two children who'd had bone surgeries but were otherwise healthy, as well as a fit young man admitted with a bad sinus infection. He was not doing well at all.

When Eve raised the issue at her team meeting that day, Dr. Saltas leaped from his chair. "We've got to refocus this whole project," he nearly shouted. "Why didn't we see this before? It's got to be one or more of the antibiotics we have been using. We've got to go through the whole pharmacy and pinpoint where this is coming from. *C. diff* only gets traction when the normal flora are wiped out of the gut."

Dr. Leron picked up on this. "He's right. There are hundreds of different kinds of antibiotics in those cabinets, and some of them could be the problem.

>>> monitor & control

"Antibiotics kill good germs along with the bad," Dr. Leron explained for the people who still looked confused. "When they kill too many good germs, a strong germ called C. diff moves into your intestine and takes over. That can make you very ill. So we have to figure out which drugs might be causing the problem."

> "Those who govern, having much business on their hands, do not generally like to take the trouble of considering and carrying into execution new projects."
> —BENJAMIN FRANKLIN

After the meeting, Eve filled out a change request and took it to Senta, the hospital administrator. She explained the need for a complete inventory of the pharmacy to isolate the problem drugs and get them out of the system. But they would need to do more than that, she said.

"More than that?" Senta asked.

"We've never automated the pharmacy. We don't have an adequate system for tracking which drugs get prescribed for which patients. Everything is supposed to be written down, but the records are kept in huge ledgers that are full of mistakes, and it takes hours to search through them. We have got to get a system installed to control the pharmacy."

"You're talking about a lot of money. This changes the whole direction of your project."

"I know," Eve said, "but if we're going to get rid of HAIs, we've got to get prescription guidelines in place. We've got to have better control of who prescribes what to whom."

In this case, the project manager herself is asking for a major scope change. Most project leaders would go crazy if this happened to them—they live in fear of scope creep as it is—but this was scope explosion. Nevertheless, there are times when the whole scope of the project has to change because of new information.

There's a big difference between scope creep and scope discovery. As a project unfolds, you might learn things that make the original scope statement inadequate to the real need. The smart project manager doesn't pledge allegiance to the scope statement but to the outcome the project is intended to produce. To make a real difference to the spread of infection in her hospital, Eve's team has a duty to move the project in a direction that nobody anticipated.

Always, the real goal is to serve the result, not the project plan.

How can you tell if you're facing scope creep or scope discovery? Here are some guidelines:

IF THE SUGGESTED CHANGE ...	THEN YOU HAVE ...
· Adds cost and time without adding significant value for the customer · Makes the project less clear, more confusing, less focused · Provides value but can be done later as a separate project or add-on · Is motivated by politics rather than an identified need	· Scope creep
· Leads to a better way to meet the real, immediate needs of the stakeholders · Clarifies the project's purpose · Focuses the project more narrowly on a manageable solution	· Scope discovery

>>>> monitor & control

These guidelines help, but you also have to go on your feelings. As one project management expert says, "If you find you're constantly adding bulk to the scope of your project, you are drowning in scope creep. If you're adding on flourishes, bells, and whistles to the project, you may be experiencing scope creep—especially if it's not clear as to why these elements are part of the project."[8]

When deciding to adopt a change or not, you definitely don't want to be a pushover for scope creep. But how do you say no, particularly if the person who wants the change is (let's be honest) more important than you are? First, you must take the change through the filter of the constraint model. This gives you the "talking document" for your conversation with the proposer. And the Four Foundational Behaviors will help you.

- **Demonstrate respect.** It doesn't do any good to fly off the handle when you receive the change or badmouth those who brought it when they're not around. Besides, *you* are a respectful person.

- **Listen first**. Make sure you understand clearly what the change is and why the person wants to make it. Remember to go back to your key stakeholder questions to clarify.

- **Clarify expectations**. Use the project change request to identify impacts of the change on cost, timing, quality, and so forth.

- **Practice accountability**. You're accountable for carrying out the project plan as agreed, which means you have to justify adding to the plan. Make sure the stakeholders are absolutely clear on what it will mean if the plan changes the constraints involved, if any, and have them approve or deny the project change request.

Living by these principles makes it easier to say no when you should.

———

There was a candy company whose top salesman was constantly overpromising. He took a huge order for a product that required a special gluten-free formula, and the customer wanted it within sixty days. Even though the project manager worked day and night to get the formula just right, the shipment date was in jeopardy. Then the salesman came in and breathlessly announced that the customers now wanted the stuff in thirty days.

The project manager suspected that the salesman was just trying to meet an earlier revenue goal, but she practiced the Four Behaviors. She listened respectfully. Then together they worked through a change request form (while he complained she was wasting his time). The project manager asked for a little time to see if she could work this out. She did not want the salesperson to see her as "reactive" (because she was certainly feeling that way), and he was itching to get back on the phone. She knew they both needed some time.

The project manager went back to her office and shut the door. She knew this was a delicate situation. She knew the salesman did not want to upset their best revenue producer, but the whole deal was now at serious risk. She called in a couple of team members, and they brainstormed a few possible solutions, but, as she suspected, she could not guarantee fulfillment on time and with quality—her integrity was too important to her. Her next reaction was to go to her boss with this and let him handle it with the executives, but she had a fairly good relationship with this salesperson and decided to have the conversation with him directly before getting the executives involved.

She carefully but quickly explained her dilemma. The project manager shared her empathy for the salesperson, who was working so hard to meet his customer's needs. The salesperson was a little taken aback at her careful conversation, and he breathed a sigh of relief that the executives were not involved. He agreed to go back to the customer again and attempt to find some "wiggle room."

It turned out that the customers only thought "it would be nice" to get the shipment earlier in order to get it on the shelves before spring, and that they would be perfectly happy if it arrived at the original date. They did not think it would affect their sales greatly.

The Four Behaviors were the answer for this project manager, but even if you live by them you might not be able to control the project. There are times to worry, like when the direction of the project changes radically but the timeline doesn't, or vice versa. Still, you'll get the best result possible by using a project change request process and practicing the Four Behaviors.

TO SUM UP ◑

MONITOR AND CONTROL Skillset and Toolset

➤ **Skill:** Keep Stakeholders Informed about Project Status

   TOOL: Project Status Report

➤ **Skill:** Manage Scope Change Effectively

   TOOL: Project Change Request

Monitoring and Controlling the project is like driving a car. You're watching the road, making corrections as you go and looking for obstacles ahead so you can avoid them. You know where you're going, but sometimes you run into an unexpected detour. You have a lot of side roads to choose from, but it's best to keep to the main route (the "critical path"). You might change your destination, but only for a very good reason.

Driving a car isn't hard if you're focused on getting where you need to go and you know the route. Likewise, the better you scope the project up front, the easier it is to Monitor and Control. The scope statement gives you the destination, and the project plan gives you the route. Still, if you want to avoid a crash, you need to control the project.

Of course, you're not driving a car; you're leading people. Nearly all project problems are people-related, as we've seen. Although you can monitor people, you can't control them. Nor should you try. But you can

>>> monitor & control

influence them, and the best way to do that is to live by the Four Behaviors yourself. The skills and tools in this chapter are useful, but only in the context of the Four Behaviors.

There may be times when you feel so frustrated you want to tell people off, throw your phone across the room, or just quit. It won't help. "When we have no control over a problem," said Stephen R. Covey, "our responsibility is to smile, to genuinely and peacefully accept the problem and learn to live with it, even if we don't like it. In this way, we do not empower the problem to control us."[9]

CHECK YOUR LEARNING—MONITORING AND CONTROLLING THE PROJECT

✓ How do you keep stakeholders informed about project status?

✓ How do you effectively manage scope change?

CHAPTER 7

Closing the Project:
End Happily—or Just End?

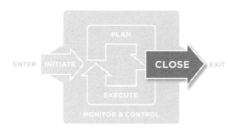

CLOSE Mindset—
Measure success and get better.

I**T WAS A COOL, SUNNY** evening in April when Carl's first Capitals event started in the university's common area. He and his team had struggled all week getting ready for it, putting up posters, buying food, and tweeting, mailing, and calling students day and night. They had dug up a French DJ and blanketed tables with éclairs and cheeses. At last the French students anxiously opened the doors, and "Paris" was open.

All the international students came, but only a few locals. Still, the kids had fun talking and dancing with each other, and to his delight, Carl watched Marta conversing happily with one of the Brazilian boys. After an hour or so, Carl told the DJ to knock off and sat down with the French kids, who were quite glum by now. They were clearly disappointed.

Carl tried to encourage them. "Maybe it will take a while before the locals feel comfortable coming to an event like this."

"It's *raté*," a French boy said. "A big fail."

Just then the French teacher, Sigi Oleson, entered. "Sorry to be late," she said as she glanced around. "Is it over already? Did you have a good turnout?"

"The Swedish. They didn't come," the French boy spoke up.

Sigi laughed. "They're Scandinavians. They're shy. They'll come around."

"I think it turned out well." Carl winked at Marta, who grinned back at him.

A few days later the director wanted a full accounting on the project, and Carl was ready for her.

"I understand it was a failure," she said, looking primly up at him.

Carl wasn't surprised by this—the director was known for her directness. "Before you make that judgment, I'd like to go through this closing checklist with you." This was a clever move because the checklist was actually the director's brainchild—remember, she was a stickler for proper procedure.

"I don't think the project is a failure," Carl said. "We've scheduled two more events for the spring term, and we've carefully documented the lessons learned, as you'll see here in our status report."

The director looked at the checklist and read the lessons learned out loud:

"We didn't get the participation from local students that we wanted. We now think advertising the event isn't sufficient, so we're taking additional measures. Professor Oleson is lobbying her department to require all foreign language students to attend the events. We've asked the student council to actively recruit people. We're announcing a drawing at the next event, 'A Night in Bangkok.' The grand prize will be a Thai massage. We think these things will make a big difference—if the students come once and see how much fun it is, they'll be back."

Carl jumped in. "Plus, we're going to publish some photos and an article about 'Paris' in the student journal." The director was silent for a while.

"By the way," he added. "There are many ways to define success." He showed her a photo he'd taken of Marta and the Brazilian boy. "Well, what do you think?"

As she gazed at the photo, Carl jumped in again. "So with your permission, I'd like to launch a new project very similar to the one we just completed. I'll do a few things differently now that I have documented lessons learned and with the term over and most of my students leaving. This means I need to build a whole new team. But we made some progress last time … I think it is worth doing again."

"All right," the director said, smiling despite herself. "Let's try it again. But I want a full accounting at term end."

Carl knew there would be no new project next academic year if he couldn't "show a return on the investment." But in his mind, there had already been a considerable return.

———

Way back in chapter one we defined a project as having a beginning and an end. There is no such thing as an ongoing project—that would be an oxymoron. So Carl is wisely getting ready to close this year's project, and then start a similar but new project next year.

THE CLOSING PROCESS

Generating, gathering, and disseminating information to formalize project completion, including evaluating the project and compiling lessons learned for use in planning future projects.

—*PMBOK* 3.3

WHY CLOSE THE PROJECT?

Closing the project is a process in itself. Of course, it means getting sign-offs on final deliveries, disbanding the team, and archiving records—that's all administrative stuff. But the most important reason for formally closing the project is to *formalize the learning.* Whether the project succeeded or not, many lessons were learned along the way—and in some cases, those lessons are the most valuable outcomes of the project, because the learning sets you up for future project success.

TOOL: CLOSING CHECKLIST

How do you know when the project is over?

It may seem the answer is obvious ("when it's done"), but you won't really know if the project is over until you go through the following checklist:

CLOSE CHECKLIST

Project Name:

Prepared by: Date:

DONE	N/A	
☐	☐	Evaluate task list.
☐	☐	Confirm fulfillment of project scope.
☐	☐	Confirm fulfillment of all Project Change Requests.
☐	☐	Complete procurement closure.
☐	☐	Document lessons learned.
☐	☐	Submit final status report to key stakeholders.
☐	☐	Seek feedback from key stakeholders.
☐	☐	Obtain all necessary sign-offs.
☐	☐	Archive project documents.
☐	☐	Publish success.
☐	☐	Celebrate project close with rewards and recognition.

Of course every project has different requirements. Some of these items won't apply to your project, but reviewing each item ensures that your project is thoroughly "done." You might want to hold a stakeholder meeting to review this checklist or just go through it yourself. Let's look closely at some of the checklist items.

>>>>> close

Evaluate Task List

This means going back over the project tasks to make sure everything has been finished. It's an inspection. Construction people call this a "punch list"; they walk through the building at the end of construction and list all the little things that still need attention. A lightbulb is missing, a screw is loose, a section of wall is still unpainted, a piece of molding isn't in place, and so forth. Usually the building contract isn't fulfilled until every item on the list is "punched" (they used to punch a little hole in the margin of the document next to a finished task).

The same is true of your project. The principle of accountability means no loose ends. If the key stakeholders don't see the need to walk through the closing process with you, ask them, "Do you want it done, or *done* done?"

————

Olivia was never happier than the day they opened the doors to the new building. With a little creative thinking from the team and the help of a new recruiting company, she had managed to fill every position without going over budget. The finance department had helped shift dollars from the relocation package and even found enough money to provide a bonus to employees who agreed to stay on and train their replacements. This solution cost far less than outsourced training and was a great morale booster. Not only was the training better and more relevant, but the employees who weren't making the move now had a reason to stay 100 percent engaged in the ongoing success of the company. Though they had a few hiccups in the early stages, Olivia had even managed to get the customer satisfaction scores to the level they'd been at before the move was announced, in part because she had communicated with customers along the way. Making them aware of the changes had been a great idea. They had been more patient and less demanding of the new team.

Days before the opening, Olivia had met with the key stakeholders to go over each of the deliverables from the project schedule. As they wrapped up the meeting, she reiterated what had been accomplished: "One hundred percent of the open positions have been filled. And though training will continue, one hundred percent of new employees have passed a skills test for their particular job. Ninety percent of the staff have already relocated, and their reimbursements have been paid. All of these employees have permanent housing. We do have a handful of people who will commute for a few more weeks, but they have all assured me they will be in the offices full-time by June fifteenth."

> "Celebrate what you've accomplished, but raise the bar a little higher each time you succeed."
> —Mia Hamm, champion pro soccer player

Olivia felt pride bubble up again as she thought back to the meeting and the impressed faces of her key stakeholders. She and her team had accomplished so much!

Samir broke through her thoughts. "You did it," he said. He gave her a congratulatory pat on the shoulder as they watched the large red ribbon fall to the ground and the doors to the new building swing open.

>>>> close

Olivia turned to grin at her new chief assistant. "*We* did it," she said.

Confirm Fulfillment of Project Scope

This is where you answer the question "Success or failure?" Did you actually fulfill the commitment you made to do everything within the scope of the project?

Here are questions to ask key stakeholders—and yourself:

- Did we meet the goals of the project?
- Are you satisfied with the end result?
- Did we deliver in a timely manner?
- Was it worth the cost?
- Did we do a good job of anticipating and mitigating risk?
- Any ideas for improving our process?

You'd think it would be easy to say if a project has succeeded or failed, but it's not. Failure, like success, is sometimes a matter of definition and who's doing the defining. Some will love it, some will be skeptical, and some will hate it. In closing a project, you have the "speed up/slow down syndrome." Imagine you're driving a tour bus through a great city—some of the tourists will want you to speed up, others want you to slow down, but most of them (the great bulging middle of the normal curve) are just happy to be there.

And if you feel like you've messed up in some respect, you're in good company. The Channel Tunnel megaproject, presumably managed by some of the most expert project leaders on the planet, went US$7 billion over budget and produced disappointing revenues for years. The US$5 billion Denver airport ended up costing US$10 billion and had only half the expected traffic the first year.[1]

Were these projects failures? One aspect of a project can fail and still produce good results. Project management methods won't completely eliminate failure, but they will help to mitigate it.

Too often project "success" is based on two measures: time and budget. Of course they matter, but another measure of success should always be whether or not you've achieved the quality desired and the business results you set out to achieve.

LESSONS LEARNED

The causes of variances, the reasoning behind the action chosen, and other types of lessons learned should be documented so they become part of the historical database for both this project and others.

—*PMBOK* 4.3.3

What if you've done the very best you can, but your project is still perceived as a "failure"? Remember the Four Foundational Behaviors. *Be respectful* by providing a safe and welcoming environment for feedback. *Listen first*, without

>>>> close

being defensive, to the people who think the project failed. Then *practice accountability*. Follow this good advice from a project manager: "Give some serious thought to what you could have done better, and deliver it to people in a way that shows that some good came of the failure, and you're a better employee for it. The 'stench of failure' is the inability to learn from mistakes."[2]

Complete Procurement Closure

In other words, make sure you've satisfied all the terms of the original project.

Did all the bills get paid? Did all of the product get delivered? Have you released other departments, vendors, consultants, and any other outside organizations from their obligations? Have you balanced the budget and reported gains or losses to the right department heads if this was your responsibility? Have all contracts been signed, approved by your legal team, and filed correctly?

These are just a few of the items that might make up your procurement closure. Every company is different. And if a contract is involved, don't leave "a couple of things to be cleaned up later," because you might not get paid. Auditors go over contracts and sign-offs, and the "couple of things" could mean payment delays, unnecessary re-work, and (worst-case scenario) lawsuits.

Document Lessons Learned

One of the top reasons for formally closing out your project is to document what you have learned along the way. To do this right, you need to do another interview—this time with your core team. It's a good idea also to invite anyone who has to live with the results. For example, if you've built a new computer program, involve the users. If it's a new system, involve operations people, and so forth.

The agenda for this interview is simple:

- What was done well?

- What needs to be done better or differently?

- What unexpected risks did we have to deal with?

- How does our process need to change to meet goals in the future?

The Four Behaviors come into play here as well. Look at the positive things *and* the negative things. Ask the team to share what went well and what could have gone better. Allow problems into the open respectfully. That means no

>>>> close

finger pointing—as project leader, *you* are accountable for the outcome—so don't punish people for raising issues. Do a lot of listening and learning without getting defensive. Your goal here is to do a project better the next time, so it's in your best interest to be quiet and hear people out. When people feel safe enough to raise opportunities for improvement, it is proof they want to play in the next game! They appreciate having a voice in the closing and are looking forward to working on the next project with you as the leader.

Submit Final Status Report to Stakeholders and Obtain Required Signatures

Like Olivia, you should call your key stakeholders together for one final meeting. Go over the task list, confirm the deliverables, and report your success and your failures. Like Carl, make your key stakeholders aware of any final steps you are taking to close the project. Strongly encourage them to make an appearance at your closing celebration to recognize the team, and last, get the signature required to document project completion.

Archive Project Documents

When we ask people in various organizations if they can find the planning documents and the documented lessons from previous projects, the overwhelming answer is "No!"

There is a story told about a man who found a bag of gold. In his excitement, he walked into the mountains, dug a hole, and hid it until he could decide how to use it. But his hiding place was too good. Though he went back into the mountains for years, he never found the gold again.

Your project documents are like gold. Imagine the riches buried in them for the next person who is assigned to a similar project. If your nugget-filled documents can't be found, their riches won't matter! Your organization should decide exactly where lessons learned and project documents will be archived. Make sure everyone has access and that projects are searchable by name and type. When you have a great archive, this will be the first place every smart project manager goes before starting a project.

Publish Your Success

Let the world know what a great team you have and what they've accomplished. Encourage the higher-ups in your organization to acknowledge team members through an email, text, card, or a company memo. You want your team to win, but you also want them to feel like winners.

Don't forget to publish your success via the proper media channels. You may want to write an article for your company newsletter or share the results with the world. Successful projects make great news stories and have powerful public relations value.

>>>> close

Celebrate Project Close with Rewards and Recognition

Celebrating is extremely important to closing a successful project. How do you show your appreciation to people who have given a lot to the project? You'll have your own style of celebrating, but you might want to remember a few things:

- People like to be thanked personally. A personal note goes a long way.

- Host a brief celebration meeting. Ensure that some or all of the key stakeholders attending are prepared to say a few words about the team's success. Have some snacks; food is a great reward. Make sure you are prepared with something nice to say about each team member. Highlight the lessons you learned in the process. Let them know you look forward to working together again on another project.

———

It wasn't quite New Year's Eve, but the hospital administration wanted to do something special for Eve's team. After all, they had done what nobody thought could be done, so the traditional Brazilian trip to the seaside for a little New Year's party wouldn't be out of line.

Almost everyone came in traditional white for the New Year. Dr. Saltas, as usual, wore his dark suit but kept his white coat on as if he were doing his rounds. As the sun set, the evening was still warm and the waves lapped on the beach. After dancing and drinks, Senta, the chief administrator, called everyone under a shady pavilion to say a few words.

"We all were skeptical when Eve set a goal of ridding our hospital of HAIs. They devastated so many of our patients, and it seemed there was nothing we could do to change the situation. We've always been strict about hygiene—almost to the point of annoying some of you"—she glanced at the doctors, who grinned back—"but we didn't really focus on the problem as we should have. Your team initiated so many excellent measures. You even have patients reminding *us* to wash our hands. You introduced new plasma filters for procedures that might put patients at risk. Most of all, you isolated an entire class of antibiotics in our pharmacy that were causing *C. diff* to thrive in our patients.

"Our HAI rates are now the lowest on the continent, and people are coming from everywhere to study how we've done it. It was always a terrible irony that people would come to us to be healed, only to become more ill than ever in our care. So many who would have suffered and perhaps even died—well, they will never know what they owe to you.

"I know Eve will be congratulating each of you personally. Everyone here contributed enormously to the results. But foremost, I want to pay tribute to Eve. She thought of this project and managed this project, and she was true to the project plan, yet flexible when required. She displayed a deep sense of accountability and respect for you, even when you didn't deserve it."

>>>>> close

Some team members raised their eyebrows. Others laughed, and Dr. Saltas pointed at himself and gave Eve a good-natured nod.

Senta concluded, "I think you will all agree Eve was a great project leader." A round of applause and even a few hoots and hollers came from the team.

"Thanks," Eve said, laughing at her team members. In the end, they'd all come together. "It was really all of you who made this possible. Thanks for sticking with me."

Everyone raised their glasses to toast.

"Just one more thing," Eve said. "I think there might be a way to solve—"

But before she could finish, someone lovingly yelled, "No more projects!" And the team ran up to hug her.

TO SUM UP ◐

CLOSE Skillset and Toolset

➤ **Skill:** Evaluate Task List

➤ **Skill:** Confirm Fulfillment of Project Scope

➤ **Skill:** Complete Procurement Closure

➤ **Skill:** Document Lessons Learned

➤ **Skill:** Submit Final Status Report to Stakeholders and Obtain Required Signatures

> **Skill:** Archive Project Documents

> **Skill:** Publish Success

> **Skill:** Celebrate Project Close with Rewards and Recognition

>> **Tool:** Closing Checklist

Check Your Learning—
Closing the Project

✓ Why close projects?

✓ How do you carry forward the lessons learned?

>>>> close

Conclusion: Your Informal Authority Is Needed Now!

A FEW FINAL THOUGHTS FROM Kory:

At the end of an intense two-day project management workshop, one participant asked for a moment of my time.

"I realized something over the past two days," he said. "I need to do more work."

"In which area?" I asked, fully expecting his answer to be technical in nature. He was a well-educated engineer with a slew of degrees and designations. I thought he would raise planning, critical path, or the Work Breakdown Structure as areas that required more focus. Instead, he looked at me sincerely and started to confess.

"I need to work on informal authority and my mastery of the Foundational Behaviors. I realized my projects are failing because I don't communicate well. I don't clarify expectations, and it *never* occurred to me that one of my biggest jobs as a project manager is to engage and inspire my team."

He paused and then looked at me again.

"Maybe I am wrong, but this is my biggest takeaway. And I can see now how leading wrong makes everything else go wrong, too."

He was one smart man.

If there is one overarching principle to successful project management, it has to be the mastery of informal authority. Learning how to lead with the Four Foundational Behaviors will be key to your success as a project manager. Yet so many of us get caught up in the tactical side of managing projects that we forget to communicate, engage the team, and measure progress toward the desired result.

Here's how another participant described the key challenge of project management:

"I have been a project manager for my whole career. I've worked on highly successful projects and very unsuccessful projects across several different companies. Here's what I've observed: Successful projects are transparent. Everyone knows what's working well and what isn't. Information is broadly shared and there's no guessing, enabling people to make small adjustments that keep the project in alignment. In unsuccessful projects, information is doled out on an 'as-needed' basis. People are expected to work in silos, keep their heads down, stay focused on their own part of the project, and are discouraged from asking questions."

Clearly, project thinking hasn't kept up with the needs of the twenty-first century. So you'll be the exceptional project manager if you use the mindsets, skillsets, and toolsets you've learned in this book.

Chances are that, as our clients have, you've figured out what you need to do to become a more effective unofficial project manager. You may need to practice clarifying expectations through key stakeholder interviews, Team Accountability Sessions, and Performance Conversations. Perhaps you need to know how to better engage your team. Or maybe you are one of the few who have mastered informal authority, but you have trouble creating and then sticking to a project plan.

Developing the skills in this book will be worth the effort, and not just for managing projects. We've said it before, and it's worth noting again, that the unofficial project management methodology has positive side effects. It complements and augments the critical time- and life-management skills you've got to have to excel in this über-paced, chaotic, and information-overloaded environment of the twenty-first century. Those skills, applied correctly, will have far-reaching effects in all areas of your life.

So what can you expect as you start to apply these skills?

You'll be more effective with people and with plans. You'll be less fearful of risk and better able to handle change. You'll ask more questions, listen better, and then you'll ask more. You'll inspire people when you hold them accountable, and you'll earn more respect. These are just a few of the outcomes you can expect when you put what you've learned in these pages to the test. Last, as you become an expert in these mindsets, skillsets, and toolsets, you will begin to notice that your projects—and your life—are moving more smoothly, and you'll create the type of momentum that can only be achieved by highly productive, highly effective people.

Unofficial project management might just be the place to be in the twenty-first-century workplace.

Glossary

Many of the following definitions originate from PMI's *Project Management Body of Knowledge.*

Acceptance Criteria: A set of conditions that must be met before deliverables are accepted.

Activity: A distinct, scheduled portion of work performed during the course of a project.

Brainstorming: A general data-gathering and creativity technique that can be used to identify risks, ideas, or solutions to issues by using a group of team members or subject matter experts.

Budget: The approved estimate for the project or any Work Breakdown Structure component or schedule activity.

Cadence of Accountability: A rhythmic process for ensuring team accountability and motivation toward weekly project commitments.

Change Control: A process whereby modifications to documents, deliverables, or baselines associated with the project are identified, documented, approved, or rejected.

Change Request: A proposal to modify any document, deliverable, or baseline.

Closing Process Group: Those processes performed to finalize all activities across all process groups and formally close a project or phase thereof.

Communication Plan: A component of the project that describes how, when, and by whom information about the project will be administered and disseminated.

Constraint: The restrictions or limitations, either internal or external, that affect the project.

Critical Path: The longest sequence of scheduled activities that must start and end as scheduled and that determine the duration of the project. If any activity on the critical path is late, the entire project will be late.

Critical Path Activity: Any activity on the critical path in a project schedule.

D.A.N.C.E.: The acronym thinking tool of *decisions, authority, need, connections,* and *energy* used to identify all key stakeholders on a project.

Deliverable: Any unique and verifiable product, result, or capability to perform a service that is required to be produced to complete a process, phase, or project.

Dependencies: A logical relationship where two activities are reliant on each other's start or finish.

Duration: The time in calendar units between the start and finish of a schedule activity. The total number of work periods (not including holidays or other nonworking periods) required to complete a schedule activity or Work Breakdown Structure component.

Early Finish Date: The specific point on the critical path method that represents the earliest possible point at which the unfinished segments of a specific schedule activity or the project as a whole can end.

Early Start Date: The specific point on the critical path that represents the earliest possible point at which the unfinished segments of a specific schedule activity or the project as a whole can begin.

Effort: The number of labor units required to complete a schedule activity or Work Breakdown Structure component, often expressed in hours, days, or weeks. Effort does not equal duration.

Estimate: A quantitative assessment of the likely amount or outcome. Usually applied to project costs, resources, effort, and durations.

Executing Process Group: Those processes required to complete the work defined in the project plan to satisfy the project specifications.

Finish-to-Finish: A logical relationship in which a successor activity cannot finish until a predecessor activity has finished.

Finish-to-Start: A logical relationship in which a successor activity cannot start until a predecessor activity has finished.

Four Foundational Behaviors: Four leadership behaviors (demonstrate respect, listen first, clarify expectations, and practice accountability) that, if mastered, will help project managers inspire the team members to want to play on their team and win.

Frontloading: The practice of expending maximum effort as early as possible to ensure a highly successful outcome and minimal risk.

Gantt Chart: A bar chart of schedule information in which activities are listed on the vertical axis, dates are shown on the horizontal axis, and activity durations are shown as horizontal bars placed according to start and finish dates.

Informal Authority: The ability to inspire team members to want to play on your team and win, even if they do not functionally report to you.

Initiating Process Group: Those processes performed to define a new project or a new phase of an existing project by obtaining authorization to start the project or phase.

Key Stakeholder: Any person who determines the success or failure of a project.

Late Finish Date: The latest date that a task can finish without delaying the finish of the project.

Late Start Date: The latest date that a task can start without delaying the finish of the project.

Lessons Learned: The knowledge gained during a project that shows how project events were addressed, or should be addressed in the future, with the purpose of improving future performance.

Lessons Learned Knowledge Base: A store of historical information and lessons learned about both the outcomes of the selection decisions and the performance of previous projects.

Logical Relationship: A dependency between two activities, or between an activity and a milestone.

Milestone: A significant point or event in a project.

Mind Mapping: A graphical brainstorming and thinking tool that improves the generation of new ideas, deliverables, components, tasks, and risks.

Monitoring and Controlling Process Group: Those processes required to track, review, and regulate the progress and performance of the project; identify any areas in which changes to the plan are required; and initiate the corresponding changes.

Most Likely Time: An estimate of the most probable activity duration that takes into account all of the known variables that could affect performance.

Optimistic Time: An estimate of the shortest activity duration that takes into account all of the known variables that could affect performance.

Organizational Project Management Maturity: The level of an organization's ability to deliver the desired strategic outcomes in a predictable, controllable, and reliable manner.

Parkinson's Law: Theory that project work "expands" to fill the time available for its completion.

Pessimistic Time: Estimate of the longest duration for an activity that takes into account all of the known variables that could affect performance.

Planning Process Group: Those processes required to establish the scope of the project, refine the objectives, and define the course of action required to attain the objectives that the project was undertaken to achieve.

Precedence Diagramming Method: A technique used for constructing a schedule model in which activities are represented by nodes and are graphically linked by one or more logical relationships to show the sequence in which the activities are to be performed.

Probability and Impact Matrix: A grid for mapping the probability of each risk occurrence and its impact on project objectives if that risk occurs.

Program Evaluation and Review Technique (PERT) Estimating: A technique for estimating duration that applies a weighted average of optimistic, pessimistic, and most likely estimates when there is uncertainty over individual activity estimates.

Project: A temporary endeavor with a start and finish undertaken to create a unique product, service, or result.

Project Management Office: An organizational structure that standardizes project-related governance processes and facilitates sharing of resources, methodologies, tools, and techniques.

Project Manager: The person assigned by the performing organization to lead the team that is responsible for achieving the project objectives.

Project Scope: The work performed to deliver a product, service, or result with the specified features and functions.

Project Scope Statement: A tool for defining the boundaries of the project; includes the project purpose, description, desired results, communication needs, constraints, exclusions, and stakeholder approvals.

Project Team: A set of individuals who support the project manager in performing the work of the project to achieve its objectives.

Resource: Skilled human resources (specific disciplines either individually or in crews or teams), equipment, services, supplies, commodities, material, budgets, or funds.

Risk: An uncertain event or condition that, if it occurs, will have a positive or negative effect on one or more project objectives.

Risk Acceptance: A risk response strategy whereby the project team decides to acknowledge the risk and not take any action unless it occurs.

Risk Elimination: A risk response strategy whereby the project team acts to eliminate the threat or protect the project from its impact.

Risk Mitigation: A risk response strategy whereby the project team acts to reduce the probability of risk or its impact.

Risk Transfer: A risk response strategy whereby the project team shifts the impact of a threat to a third party, together with ownership of the response.

Schedule: A representation of the plan for executing the project's activities, including their durations, dependencies, and other planning information, used to produce a project schedule.

Scope: The sum of the products, services, and results to be provided as a project. See also **Project Scope**.

Scope Change: Any change to the project scope. A scope change almost always requires an adjustment to the project cost or schedule.

Scope Creep: The tendency of a project to change and grow into an uncontrollable monster.

Sequence Activities: The process of identifying and documenting relationships among the project activities.

Sponsor: A person or group who provides resources and support for the project and is accountable for enabling its success.

Stakeholder: A person or an organization that is actively involved in the project or is positively or negatively impacted by it.

Start-to-Start: A logical relationship in which a successor activity cannot start until a predecessor activity has started.

TAME: The thinking tool acronym for the four areas to consider when deciding how to manage a particular risk—should the risk be *transferred, accepted, mitigated,* or *eliminated*?

Team Accountability Session: A brief and motivating meeting with the sole intent of letting the team evaluate the overall project to see if they are winning or losing. Each team member commits to one or two responsibilities that will keep the project on track for that week. Everyone plays to win together.

Work: The amount of effort (minutes, hours, days) needed to accomplish a task.

Work Breakdown Structure (WBS): A hierarchy of project deliverables and their associated components reflecting the total scope of work to be carried out by the project team to accomplish the project objectives.

NOTES

Chapter One

[1] PMI's *Pulse of the Profession®: The High Cost of Low Performance 2013* (Newtown Square, PA: Project Management Institute, 2013), 2, 4–5, 8.

[2] Ibid., 15.

[3] Seth Godin, *Tribes: We Need You to Lead Us* (New York: Penguin, 2008), 29–30.

[4] *Closing the Gap: The Link Between Project Management Excellence and Long-Term Success* (London: The Economist Intelligence Unit, 2009), 10.

[5] Ray Ahern, "The Case for KISS: Keeping It Simple in a Complex Environment," *Bright Hub PM*, May 29, 2013, http://www.bright hubpm.com/project-planning/123887-the-case-for-kiss-keeping -it-simple-in-a-complex-environment/.

[6] *A Guide to the Project Management Body of Knowledge (PMBOK® Guide)*, 5th ed. (Newtown Square, PA: Project Management Institute, 2013).

Chapter Two

[1] Harold R. Kerzner, *Project Management: A Systems Approach to Planning, Scheduling, and Controlling* (Hoboken, NJ: Wiley, 2013), 73–74.

[2] "Disengaged Employees," *Stupid IT Project Managers,* May 17, 2012, http://stupid-it-project-managers.blogspot.com/2012/05 /disengaged-employees.html.

[3] Stephen R. Covey, *The 7 Habits of Highly Effective People* (New York: Simon & Schuster, 2013), 195.

[4] Elisabeth Bucci, "If You Can't Do This, You Can't Be a Project Manager," *The Passionate Project Manager* (blog), June 13, 2013, http://www.thepassionateprojectmanager.com/2013/06/13/il -you-cant-do-this-you-cant-be-a-project-manager/.

[5] Gretchen Gavett, "The Hidden Indicators of a Failing Project," *HBR Blog Network*, October 23, 2013, http://blogs.hbr .org/2013/10/the-hidden-indicators-of-a-failing-project.

[6] *PMI's Pulse of the Profession®*, 8.

Chapter Three

[1] Emily Sohn, "People Naturally Walk in Circles," *Discovery News*, August 19, 2009, http://news.discovery.com/human/evolution /walking-circles.htm.

[2] Ralph Kliem, *Effective Communications for Project Management* (Boca Raton, FL: CRC Press, 2008), 31.

[3] *PMBOK* 5.2.3.1.

[4] Covey, *7 Habits*, 101.

[5] Seth Godin, "The Three Toxic Stooges of the Project Apocalypse," *Seth's Blog*, November 19, 2013, http://sethgodin.typepad .com/seths_blog/2013/11/the-three-toxic-stooges-of-the-project -apocalypse.html.

Chapter Four

[1] David A. Zimmer, "Four Logical Relationships of Project Management: What They Are and How to Use Them," *The Project Professor's Personal PM Tutor*, January 21, 2011, http://terms.ameagle .com/2011/01/four-logical-relationships-of-project.html.

[2] Spark KD, "Living with Parkinson's Law," *Bright Hub PM*, May 22, 2011, http://www.brighthubpm.com/project-planning/58631 -living-with-parkinsons-law/.

[3] "Project Management Disasters," *Angry 365 Days a Year* (blog), April 21, 2008, http://angryaussie.wordpress.com/2008/04/21 /project-management-disasters/.

[4] "PERT," *NetMBA Knowledge Center*, accessed October 11, 2014, http://www.netmba.com/operations/project/pert/.

[5] Kerzner, *Project Management*, 269.

Chapter Five

[1] Joe Knight, Roger Thomas, and Brad Angus, "The Dirty Little Secret of Project Management," *Harvard Business Review Blog Network,* March 11, 2013, http://blogs.hbr.org/2013/03/the-dirty -little-secret-of-pro/.

[2] Joe Knight, Roger Thomas, and Brad Angus, *Project Management for Profit: A Failsafe Guide to Keeping Projects on Track and on Budget* (Boston: Harvard Business Review Press, 2012), 9.

[3] Godin, "Three Toxic Stooges."

[4] Grant M. Howe, cited in Jennifer Lonoff Schiff, "13 Tips for Keeping IT Projects under Control," *CIO,* March 18, 2013, http:// www.cio.com/article/2387513/project-management/13-tips-for -keeping-it-projects-under-control.html.

[5] Brené Brown, *The Gifts of Imperfection: Let Go of Who You Think You're Supposed to Be and Embrace Who You Are* (Center City, MN: Hazelden, 2010), 19.

[6] Knight et al., *Project Management for Profit,* 163.

Chapter Six

[1] Michael D. Taylor, *How to Monitor a Project,* 2009, 3, http://www .itbusinessedge.com/itdownloads/project-management-toolkit /88691.

[2] S. F. Seay, "Stupid Things Project Managers (and Others) Say!" *Project Steps* (blog), February 14, 2005, http://projectsteps .blogspot.com/2005/02/stupid-things-project-managers-and .html.

[3] Cited in Gavett, "The Hidden Indicators."

[4] Knight et al., "Dirty Little Secret."

[5] Taylor, *How to Monitor a Project,* 2.

[6] Knight et al., *Project Management for Profit,* 143.

[7] Laurence Baynham, cited in Sylvia Pennington, "Seven Signs Your Project Is Heading for Disaster," *Sydney Morning Herald,* July 25, 2012, http://www.smh.com.au/it-pro/business-it/seven-signs -your-project-is-headed-for-disaster-20120725-22p20.html.

[8] Ronda Bowen, "That Might Actually Be Scope Creep! Test Your Knowledge of the Difference between Scope Creep and Discovery," *Bright Hub PM,* October 12, 2011, http://www.brighthubpm

.com/project-planning/124396-test-your-knowledge-of-the
-difference-between-scope-creep-and-discovery.
[9] Covey, *7 Habits*, 86.

Chapter Seven

[1] Bent Flyvbjerg, Nils Bruzelius, and Werner Rothengatter, *Megaprojects and Risk: An Anatomy of Ambition* (Cambridge, UK: Cambridge University Press, 2003), 3.
[2] "How Do I Survive a Failed Project?" *The Workplace Stack Exchange,* May 10, 2013, http://workplace.stackexchange.com/questions/11712/how-do-i-survive-a-failed-project.

INDEX

Bold refers to definition.

ABOUT THE AUTHORS

KORY KOGON is FranklinCovey's Global Practice Leader for Productivity, focusing her research and content development around time, project management, and communication skills. She is one of the authors of *The 5 Choices: The Path to Extraordinary Productivity*, *Project Management Essentials for the Unofficial Project Manager*, and *Presentation Advantage*.

Kory brings more than twenty-five years of business expertise from frontline positions to being an executive team member. Prior to FranklinCovey, Kory spent six years as the Executive Vice President of Worldwide Operations for AlphaGraphics, Inc. She was responsible for the teams and projects that helped franchisees start up their business, develop staff, and reach profitability. She led the implementation of ISO 9000 globally, and managed the installation of the first company-wide global learning system.

In 2005 *Utah Magazine* honored Kory as one of the "Top 30 Business Women to Watch" in Utah.

In 2012 Kory earned a Certificate in the Foundations of NeuroLeadership from the NeuroLeadership Institute, of which she is an ongoing member.

SUZETTE BLAKEMORE joined FranklinCovey in 2012 as a Regional Productivity Practice leader, a role in which she brings concrete understanding to myriad organizations and individuals on the productivity challenges facing workforces today.

Prior to joining FranklinCovey, Suzette spent more than twenty years in the corporate world, moving from being a top-producing sales person to an executive team member.

Suzette is a Certified Franchise Executive and has held additional certifications from the Direct Marketing Association and the Association for Talent Development. She currently serves as an honorary board member for the EcSell Institute.

Suzette resides in Salt Lake City, Utah, with her husband, John, their three children (Chelsie, Mariesa, and Christian), and her Husky/Malamute mix, Kayak. She loves to scuba dive, read, write, and travel.

JAMES WOOD is a senior leadership consultant and coach with FranklinCovey; he has dual bases in Denver, Colorado, and Honolulu, Hawaii. He has more than twenty-five years of diverse leadership experience with project management, software development, engineering, operations, and training organizations.

James holds a Doctor of Business Administration degree from the University of Phoenix School of Advanced Studies along with a master's degree in Computer Information Systems from Regis University and a master's degree in Environmental Policy and Management from the University of Denver. He has been certified as a Project Management

Professional through the Project Management Institute since 1998, and is a Associate Certified Coach (ACC) with the International Coach Federation.

James is an adjunct professor at four universities, teaching undergraduate, master's, and doctoral students in business. He often speaks on issues of leadership trust, project management, and leadership greatness. He has two extraordinary adult children: Kimberly, a marine biologist and photographer, and Vincent, an airline pilot.

ABOUT FRANKLINCOVEY

FranklinCovey Co. (NYSE:FC) is a global company specializing in performance improvement. We help organizations achieve results that require a change in human behavior. Our expertise is in seven areas: leadership, execution, productivity, trust, sales performance, customer loyalty, and education. FranklinCovey clients have included 90 percent of the Fortune 100, more than 75 percent of the Fortune 500, thousands of small- and mid-sized businesses, as well as numerous government entities and educational institutions. FranklinCovey has more than 40 direct and licensee offices providing professional services in over 140 countries. For more information, visit www.franklincovey.com.

PROJECT MANAGEMENT ESSENTIALS

You can take your Project Management skills to the next level by:

- Participating in an Executive Overview webcast to see how a *Project Management Essentials for the Unofficial Project Manager* work session would impact your team or organization
- Connecting with a FranklinCovey client partner to diagnose productivity issues and learn about the variety of work sessions that are available to meet specific needs.

Visit http://pm.franklincovey.com for more information or all 1-888-576-1776.

FranklinCovey's Productivity Practice helps individuals and organizations master the three key competencies required for peak performance:

- Methodically invest valuable time, attention, and energy on the highest priorities (*The 5 Choices to Extraordinary Productivity*—visit www.the5choices.com).

- Complete projects on time, on budget, and with the highest quality (*Project Management Essentials for the Unofficial Project Manager*—visit http://pm.franklincovey.com).
- Powerfully inform and persuade one person or one hundred, face-to-face or virtually (*Presentation Advantage*—visit http://presentation.franklincovey.com).

The mindsets, skillsets, and toolsets of the Productivity Suite work together, enabling knowledge workers and leaders to perform at their peak and feel more accomplished every day.

Visit http://productivity.franklincovey.com for more information or call 1-888-576-1776.